**T5-AFT-504**

Here's what they're saying...

"A systematic approach by prolific and knowledgeable expert Rodnay Zaks..."
Mechanix Illustrated

"The (microcomputer) buyer ought to bone up by reading...(this book)."
Business Week

"A good book to read before going to the stores to check out the merchandise (and to take with you when you go)."
In Business

"Spend a few bucks on this book, and you can save yourself a lot of money and grief when you go pick out your first microcomputer. That is to say that (this book) succeeds both in explaining computers and in explaining how to get your money's worth when you buy one."
Electronic Field Engineer

"All will profit from this presentation of the essentials of personal and business computing and computer systems."
Boston Computer Update

"Very helpful to anyone who is considering purchasing a microcomputer."
Mathematics Teacher

"Rodnay Zaks' latest offering is refreshingly clear. (It) gives the reader a good feel for the subject."
Practical Computing

"An excellent book for anyone new to computing...who is considering a microcomputer for either personal or business use."
On Computing

"A good introduction to all the elements of a real computer system... for the businessman who wants to learn the ABC's of microcomputers."
Computer Retailing

"Author Rodnay Zaks fulfills his promise to present a practical, progressive introduction. Clear, comprehensive...practical."
Kilobaud Microcomputing

YOUR FIRST COMPUTER

A Guide to Business and Personal Computing

YOUR FIRST COMPUTER

A Guide to Business and Personal Computing

RODNAY ZAKS

The first edition of
this book was published under the title:
**AN INTRODUCTION TO PERSONAL
AND BUSINESS COMPUTING**

CP/M is a trademark of Digital Research
NAD is a trademark of Structured Systems
Wordstar is a trademark of Micropro International
TRS-80 is a trademark of Tandy
Apple II is a trademark of Apple
PET is a trademark of Commodore
Etc. Almost all software and computer names mentioned in this book are manufacturer trademarks and should be treated as such.

Graphics by Daniel Le Noury

Every effort has been made to supply complete and accurate information. However, Sybex assumes no responsibility for its use, nor for any infringements of patents or other rights of third parties which would result. No license is granted by the equipment manufacturers under any patent or patent rights. Manufacturers reserve the right to change circuitry at any time without notice.

In particular, technical characteristics and prices are subject to rapid change. Comparisons and evaluations are presented for their educational value and for guidance principles. The reader is referred to the manufacturer's data for exact specifications.

Copyright © 1980, SYBEX Inc. World Rights reserved. No part of this publication may be stored in a retrieval system, copied, transmitted, or reproduced in any way, including but not limited to, photocopy, photography, magnetic or other recording, without the prior agreement and written permission of the publisher.

Library of Congress Card Number: 80-51036
1st Edition published 1978. 2nd Edition published 1980.
ISBN 0-89588-045-8
Printed in the United States of America
10 9 8 7 6 5

Contents

14 TOMORROW 229

Conclusion. Tomorrow. Summary.

Appendices

Illustrations

Preface

The purpose of this book is to explain what a microcomputer is, how it works, and what it can do, depending upon your intended application and budget.

After reading *Your First Computer,* you should be able to decide whether you should use a computer, and if so, which one, and with which peripherals. This book was written for the individual considering the use or purchase of a small computer. Neither a technical background nor a prior knowledge of computers is required.

Progress in the miniaturization of electronic circuits has resulted in the availability of powerful small computers at very low cost. These small computers may be used effectively for business or personal applications, provided that their limitations, as well as your own, are understood. In particular, the selection of peripherals and programs is often more important than the choice of the computer itself. Although the criteria for selection appear complex, this book will prove that they are, in fact, quite simple, provided that the limitations imposed by any selection are understood.

All of the information required to understand the elements of a computer system, including the hardware, the programs, and the human considerations is presented in fourteen chapters. Each chapter has been designed to be as easy to read as possible. Many topics are simplified, and references for the avid reader are offered at the end of the book.

This book has been designed so that all the concepts and vocabulary are presented and defined before they are used. Reading each chapter in sequence is, therefore, advisable.

The first three chapters of *Your First Computer* introduce you to the world of microcomputers. You will speak ROM and RAM, and even "use" a system, so that you can better understand the functions of its components.

If you want to understand how the system works, Chapter 4 takes you inside the box and describes the functions of the system in detail. If you want to program the computer, you will have a choice between two techniques: assembly language and high-level language. Chapters 5 and 6 introduce you to these programming languages, from BASIC to PASCAL.

At this point, you should be familiar with the hardware and software components of a computer system, but you will not yet have had an opportunity to use them together. Chapter 7 presents actual sessions with the computer. Two typical business applications are demonstrated: a mailing list program and a word processing program. The specific requirements of business computing are then analyzed and explained.

Having acquired an understanding of computers and the requirements imposed by specific applications, the time has come to select one. The general criteria for choosing a computer system are presented in Chapter 8. These criteria will be applied to existing devices, peripherals, and computers.

One of the most significant factors from a cost standpoint may not be the microcomputer box itself, but the peripherals. Chapter 9 explains the different types of peripherals, which one should be used in specific circumstances, and why.

Chapter 10 presents the main computers on the market today, and discusses their characteristics in terms of their intended uses.

Knowing, at this point, what to use, the next question is: should you buy a system now? Chapter 11 addresses this question, and explores alternatives for the business user.

Human limitations are a significant aspect when considering the use of a computer. The pitfalls awaiting the business user are many, and they are described in Chapter 12 ("How to Fail").

Some help is available and is discussed in Chapter 13 ("Help").

Finally, predicting the future can be attempted on a limited scale, and a perspective is presented in Chapter 14.

Technically-minded readers will find additional information in the Appendix section of this book.

1

THE MICROCOMPUTER ERA

At Home

It is 7:00 a.m. The alarm buzzes softly in the room. Jim wakes up and stops the alarm. A miniature television display tube lights up close to the bed and displays a message. "CHECK THE RV FILE BEFORE LEAVING." Jim gets up. Before leaving the bedroom he silently punches two keys on his bedside keyboard: "BR." This is a breakfast order, which will automatically start the coffee machine and heat up the doughnuts that Jim likes in the morning. Confirmation appears on the small television-like display by the bedside: "COFFEE STARTED. WILL HEAT TWO DOUGHNUTS."

Jim now proceeds to his study in order to check the file, as requested. As he walks through the house, the lights turn on automatically, in sequence, as he passes through corridors and rooms.

Jim reaches his study. The "RV" file is already displayed for him on the large television terminal sitting on his desk. It lists two new appointments that were made for him in the office after he left. He finds out that an "override message" was left by his supervisor during the evening, urgently requesting him to attend a special sales meeting at 9:00 this morning. Jim makes a note of his new appointment schedule, and nervously questions his home microcomputer system to find out who else will be attending the sales meeting. Unfortunately, the meeting attendance list, which has been filed by his supervisor, is being protected against unauthorized reading, and may not be displayed on the screen. Jim gets up and simply decides to hurry and arrive at the office early. His breakfast is already prepared and waiting for him. The heater for the house has been automatically turned on, making the breakfast room pleasantly warm.

Jim eats quickly, while his wife and children sleep on. As soon as he is finished, he punches the kitchen keyboard for his car. The garage door opens and the car engine is automatically turned on. Jim goes back to

the main terminal in the study, and connects to the house computer of two of his colleagues. He finds that they have all already checked into the office. He decides to leave quickly. He goes to the garage, where the engine of his car is now warm, and drives away. The lights in the house automatically shut off as he exits. A similar morning routine will occur half an hour later when his wife wakes up.

Jim is now in his car and would like to get to his office as quickly as possible. He punches his car keyboard to interrogate the main city traffic computer. He is informed of a recommended detour through a side street, that should decrease the amount of time he will need to get to his office. Unfortunately, Jim is not familiar with the recommended itinerary. He requests assistance. His car computer now examines the street sensors, and automatically displays the turns he must take to follow the desired path. His car display is now flashing "TURN RIGHT NEXT INTERSECTION." Jim follows the instructions. He quickly checks his mileage computer, which displays another twelve miles to go with an estimated twenty-two minutes travel time. Jim feels better now: he will be arriving at the office in plenty of time for his meeting. He does not have to worry about any obvious malfunction. His car computer already tested the engine while it was warming up, and determined that all functional components were in satisfactory condition. His mileage computer also determined that the amount of gas remaining in the tank is sufficient for the usual distance.

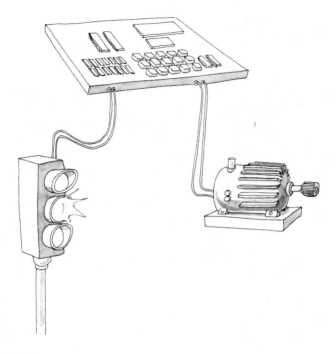

At the Office

Jim now arrives at his office. At the entrance, he places his palm on a special rectangular frame equipped with a sensor, and the door opens. Jim has been identified by the security computer, which records his entry at the same time. On his desk, Jim finds a computer printout listing the points to be covered at the 9:00 sales meeting. Now aware of the goal of the meeting, he immediately proceeds to his personal terminal, where he requests a printout of the relevant data files he would like to refer to during the meeting. The attendance file has now been unlocked, and Jim displays it on his television screen to find out who else will attend. An update appears on the screen: the meeting is postponed for fifteen minutes. Jim decides to call his colleague Peter to discuss the results of their project. He places the call. A small display simultaneously lights up on his telephone, and an incoming message flashes: "MR. GOR-VIN FROM PRECISE SYSTEMS INC. IS CALLING." Jim pushes the "deny" button. His secretary has been automatically advised that he does not wish to answer the call at this time. The silent display of the incoming message allowed him to make an immediate decision without interrupting the conversation with his colleague. He finishes his conversation and then goes to the meeting room.

At the Hospital

During this time, his wife, Linda, who now works mostly at home as an architect, decides to visit her relative Jane. She drives to the hospital. At the hospital, the receptionist types in Linda's name on the reception terminal, and the name is accepted, indicating that the visit is approved, both in terms of hospital regulations, and doctor approval for visits. The number of her friend's room appears on the display: "ROOM 305 ON THE THIRD FLOOR." She proceeds to the room. Jane has had a serious operation, and is now on automatic monitoring. Special probes continuously monitor her vital functions, such as her heart beat, blood pressure, brain activity, respiratory rate and temperature. These sensors are connected to the bedside microcomputer which continuously checks the measured values against limits set by the physician, and combinations that might indicate a bodily malfunction. So far, all of the vital signs have been normal. However, during the night the heart monitoring program in the room next door detected an arythmia, which is likely to occur before an actual heart attack. The early warning signal awakened Jane, who heard the physician rush into the room and immediately undertake medical action to prevent the possible heart failure. The intervention was completely successful, and the attack was prevented.

Jane explains to Linda that when she leaves the hospital, her heart condition will have to be monitored for a period of at least two months. She has decided to follow the advice of her physician and rent a portable unit from the hospital. This unit would give her an early signal, should a possible malfunction be detected by the portable microcomputer. In addition, every evening, she will have to connect her portable microcomputer to the telephone, and allow it to transmit the data collected during the day to the hospital computer, which will then run a sophisticated analysis program to diagnose either progress toward recovery, or signs of complications. All of Jane's medications are not monitored by her bedside computer, but by a large hospital computer, which checks any physician's prescription for Jane against the list of other medications she is already using, and the list of medications to which she may be allergic. Any potentially dangerous combination is immediately flagged to the attention of the attending physician.

Jane, who is a very active person, brought her personal microcomputer into her room in order to keep working on the report that she has been preparing for the past week. She can use her microcomputer to communicate with libraries, and examine the contents of sections of books that she wants to consult. She can then pursue her work toward the report at her own pace.

She is careful not to use her microcomputer for too long, for her doctor has forbidden any work for periods of more than three hours per day. Once she has used the permissible three hours, her personal microcomputer is automatically disconnected by the monitoring computer.

Back Home

Linda now drives back home where she intends to quickly take care of some household chores and resume her architecture work. Upon arrival, she consults her personal microcomputer for a listing of urgent things to do for the day. It appears that she has to transfer money from her savings account, as her checking account is almost depleted. In addition, a number of household bills will be overdue within a day. She decides to take care of that first. Connecting to the banking computer, she orders the appropriate transfers to be made from her account to her creditor's account. For each transaction, she types a special identification code, which verifies the author of the transaction and its validity. Next, she connects to her favorite store's computer to specify delivery of a list of items. However, she is undecided this morning as to which vegetables and fruits to buy. She requests a visual display of the merchandise available, and a listing of prices. On her television screen, the available fruits and vegetables are displayed together with their prices. She makes a few notes, and then specifies the rest of her shopping list. It will be delivered by 4:00 this afternoon, as specified in the rectangle at the top of her television screen.

Linda has now taken care of her immediate needs for the day, and decides to work for an hour on her language lesson. She is learning Spanish. A conversation in Spanish fills the room. The sounds are generated by the program, via a voice synthesizer. At the same time, the corresponding written text appears on her terminal. She is asked to repeat the words. Every time that she fails to provide a satisfactory imitation of the sound, the program repeats the previous sentence until it receives a satisfactory sound imitation, or after she has made five attempts. The program continues in sequence, putting Linda through a series of exercises. After an hour, Linda decides to stop, have lunch, and then get to work on her architectural drawings. Before turning the terminal off temporarily, she specifies a list of events that may automatically trigger the house sound system in the kitchen. She allows news from her husband, Jane at the hospital, her children, her boss, as well as the latest news report on a political election. She then goes into the kitchen and prepares her lunch.

Later, Linda works in her room, drawing architectural plans on a special tablet, displaying them on the screen, and then correcting errors with the aid of her computer. When the plans have been sufficiently finalized, she will transmit them to her office computer, where they will be examined and criticized or approved by her boss.

When Linda finishes her work, the screen lights up, and two messages flash on it — two of her neighbors have called during the afternoon, but were prevented from interrupting her work. They left messages, which were stored in the memory of the system.

The children will soon come back from school, and use Linda's computer to prepare their homework. Linda hopes to buy her elder daughter her own computer soon.

The Electronic City

All of the microcomputers in Jim's house, as well as in other houses, offices, hospitals, and buildings are interconnected through complex networks. Immediate information is available at any time to all who are authorized to access it. All information transfer is virtually instantaneous, and can be performed from any terminal, within the house, car, or office.

Work patterns have been radically changed. Fewer people work at an office, unless they need to personally relate to one of their colleagues, or use special resources. Most people now work directly from their homes on tasks that can be performed with the assistance of a terminal. Work has become more efficient and creative, resulting in a shorter work week.

Most tasks (manual or automated) are now performed and monitored by miniature microcomputers. Even the familiar wristwatch has become a small microcomputer equipped with a miniature keyboard and display that can be used to communicate with other microcomputers.

When?

The above scenario was fiction. When will it be a reality? All of the facilities described above can be technically implemented today. Simply for economic reasons, they have not yet been utilized on a large scale, and are not available at a low enough cost. We can, however, safely predict that a large number of them will be implemented within the next decade. And, many improvements will be available that cannot even be imagined at this point. The purpose of the previous text was to suggest the variety of applications now possible with the advance of microcomputers.

Microcomputers

Microcomputers are the result of astonishing progress in MOS (Metal Oxide Semiconductor) technology, which made it possible to implement a complete computer on a small rectangle of silicon (a "chip," approximately 5 x 5 millimeters). The functions previously performed by large computers occupying an entire room can now be performed by single-chip microcomputers.

The microcomputer is rapidly becoming an increasingly important part of society. Recent developments have made the microcomputer an indispensable tool for home and business.

Let us now learn to use Jim's or Linda's microcomputer, today. This book will present various applications and utilization techniques.

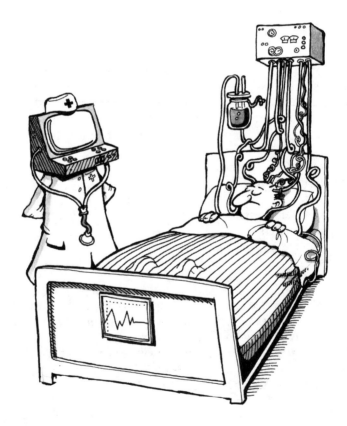

2

USING THE SYSTEM

INTRODUCTION

We have just acquired a microcomputer system: it includes a microcomputer box, a television-like display with a keyboard, and an ordinary cassette recorder. While additional options are available that may be used with this system, we will not review them until later chapters. The purpose of this chapter is to help you understand the main elements of a system by showing you how to use them.

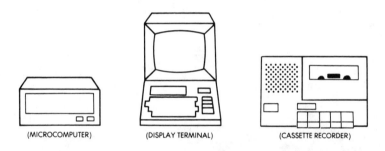

(MICROCOMPUTER)   (DISPLAY TERMINAL)   (CASSETTE RECORDER)

Figure 2-1:   A personal microcomputer system

CONNECTING THE SYSTEM

We are now eager to just "do something" with our microcomputer system. Let us connect it. We have three modules and three cables. Let us first discuss the modules. They are:

1. The microcomputer box which executes programs.
2. The television-like display with a keyboard, called a CRT terminal. ("CRT" stands for Cathode Ray Tube, which is identical to a TV tube; "terminal" indicates that it includes a keyboard as well as certain required processing functions.)

3. The cassette player which is a standard audio-cassette player. (The cassette player with our system has a simple counter and a remote-control jack.)

Now let us connect the system with the three cables. First, let us connect the CRT terminal to the microcomputer. The standard interconnect cable is terminated by "RS-232" connectors, which plug into the CRT at one end, and the microcomputer at the other. Almost all microcomputers and CRT terminals have this standard RS-232 interface. However, microcomputers that integrate the display within the microcomputer box may not require it (for example, PET).

Connecting the tape recorder requires a special cable, which is plugged into the mike input, the external speaker output, the remote-control socket on the recorder side, and a special socket on the microcomputer side.

Now, let us turn everything on. The microcomputer is turned on with an on/off key. We turn it on, and the "ON" light appears. Next, the CRT terminal is turned on, and a white square appears on the screen. This square is a "cursor" that indicates the next position at which the microcomputer will display a character on the screen. We hit "reset" on the CRT keyboard, and the cursor moves to the top left of the screen. This is where we (or the microcomputer) will start "writing on the screen."

Figure 2-2: This system integrates the keyboard in the microcomputer box.

Figure 2-3: Hitting a key on the keyboard sends a binary code to the microcomputer.

We now hit any key on the keyboard. The computer responds immediately: "READY" appears on the screen. The system is now ready to accept commands from us, and will wait indefinitely.

When we hit the key on the keyboard, the closure was detected by keyboard electronics, and converted into a standard "binary code" called ASCII (which will be explained later). The microprocessor received a signal requesting it to read the character. The character was then promptly read via the RS-232 interconnect cable. In this instance, the action taken by the computer did not depend on the character: any character would have caused the computer to display "READY".

Now, on the screen we see the letter "A," which we just hit (this is called the "echo-back" from the computer), on the line below the word "READY".

Figure 2-4: The microcomputer responds

Note: the microcomputer actually had to send two additional characters to the display, to insure that "READY" would not appear on the same line as "A." The first character is called a "line feed": the cursor moved down one line. The second character is called a "carriage return": the cursor moved to the left-most position on the screen, below the "A." Only then was the word "READY" sent.

This "echo-back" is an important feature of a computer. It is not included in a traditional typewriter, where a letter is printed as soon as a key is pressed. In a computer terminal, whether a teletype or a CRT display, a character is printed or displayed by the computer. This process offers two advantages:

1. Verification of error-free transmission. Seeing the "A" appear on the screen verifies that it has been properly read by the computer, and that the communication cable is operating correctly in both directions.

2. Interpretation of a character. For example, in a business sytem, a password may be required before anyone can use the system. (Let us assume that the password is "HENRY8.") It would be important that the password is not echoed-back; it would obviously be an error to have the password displayed on the screen as it is typed. Any good system will insure that this does not happen.

Now that we have learned about our system, let's use it to play a game.

PLAYING A GAME

We begin by loading a program into the system from a cassette, in order to play a game of tic-tac-toe with the computer. It is necessary to load the program into the computer each time, since the computer's main memory is volatile, that is, its contents disappear when the power is turned off. (This is an unfortunate drawback of the LSI technology used to achieve such microminiaturization and low cost.) The programs are permanently stored on a magnetic storage device such as the cassette, which is not affected by power being on or off.

After the system is turned on, the program, residing on the cassette, will be transferred into the central memory of the system so that it can be executed. The user, sitting at the keyboard, will type the necessary instructions from the user manual and transfer the program called "tic-tac-toe" to the central memory of the system. The actual sequence depends upon the manufacturer.

We now type a command: "LOAD TCTO FROM TAPE," and the board layout of nine squares appears on the CRT display. We are now

ready to play. We enter our moves, which provide data to the program. The program will then respond.

In this example, data are entered by specifying into which square we want to enter an "X" (in this particular program, the computer always plays with an "O," and we always have an "X"). We will play in the center of the board. We specify "2-2," which are the coordinates of row 2 and column 2. We terminate our input with a "carriage return," a special character analogous to the one on the electric typewriter. This special character is used to tell the program: "I have finished typing my input. Please process."

This program is fairly fast, and after just a second of "thinking," the computer responds. A circle appears in position 1-1. It is now our turn to respond. The game proceeds in the obvious manner, until either we win or the computer wins. The tic-tac-toe program is a fairly simple program that executes efficiently, i.e., responds quickly. If we wanted to play a game like chess, against an "intelligent" program, then the response of the computer would be much slower, as it would need to execute a long program before "knowing" what to do.

Thus far, we have illustrated the function of the *input device* (the keyboard through which we have supplied data to the computer). We have also shown the function of the *computer*, which executed the tic-tac-toe program, read the data provided, and displayed the response.

We have also illustrated the role of the CRT display as an *output device*. The screen was used by the computer to display the moves of the game.

Finally, a tape has been used as a *long term storage* device for programs we want to keep after the power is turned off.

If we want to play a new game, for example, a game of NIM, we must execute a different program. To do so we would type another sequence of commands at the keyboard, and load a different program into the memory.

At the end of this particular game, the computer displays:

"WANT ANOTHER GAME?"

We answer "NO."

The computer displays: "READY."

It has reverted to "executive" or "monitor" mode, where it does nothing else but wait indefinitely for user commands.

Now, let us load another program and test our skills with the multiplication table.

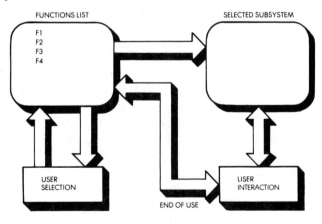

FUNCTIONS LIST

F1
F2
F3
F4

SELECTED SUBSYSTEM

USER SELECTION

USER INTERACTION

END OF USE

Figure 2-5:   The system proposes a "menu" of programs

ANOTHER PROGRAM

In order to load this new program, we type:

"LOAD MATH FRON TAPE"

followed by a "carriage return." The carriage return is an "attention" signal for the microcomputer, signifying that our message is complete, and that the computer can process it.

This time, however, our message does not work:

"ERROR ABOVE. PLEASE REENTER"

The computer will accept only specific commands. The correct command is "LOAD . . . FROM . . ." The typing error in "FRON" has been automatically detected.

Yes, an "intelligent computer" should understand that we meant "FROM," not "FRON." Unfortunately, the complexity necessary to accept partially incorrect commands is such that no small or medium sized computer is designed to do so—it is simply not worth the additional cost.

So, we must reenter the command:

"LOAD MATH FROM TAPE" (Carriage Return)   r

The statement is now accepted, and the computer answers:

"SEARCHING MATH..."

Had we noticed the typing error immediately, we could have used an important facility available on our CRT terminal: "text-editing." We simply hit a special key, the "left arrow," and the cursor moves left by one character. We continue moving it back until it is over the "N" of FRON, and then we type "M." "M" is automatically substituted for "N." We then move the cursor right by hitting the special key "right arrow," and proceed.

Note that, at a minimum, any VDT (Video Display Terminal) lets you move the cursor in all directions, so that errors can be conveniently corrected (or additional data entered).

Now let us go back to our cassette recorder. We press "FAST FORWARD," and it starts moving. Pressing the "forward" key is an inconvenience that can be eliminated by the use of more expensive peripherals, such as disks. We stop the tape at 550 on the counter, and wait, while several curious words appear on the screen:

NIM . . .
CHEK . . .
STOK . . .

The microcomputer is searching the tape for our program. Finally, the magic word appears:

"MATH FOUND"

and after a delay:

READY-SPECIFY

1 - FOR MULTIPLICATION

2 - FOR DIVISION

3 - FOR ADDITION

4 - FOR SUBTRACTION

ENTER YOUR CHOICE . . .

The reason that the computer took so long is that we stopped the tape at 550 on the counter, so as not to "overshoot," and the microcomputer read all the intermediate programs before finding ours. If there was no counter, a long period of time could pass before our "MATH" program is found. But we have now located it. Let us illustrate some of its features.

This time, the program starts by displaying a "MENU" offering four possibilities: multiplication, division, addition, subtraction. We enter: "1" (for multiplication), and then a "carriage return."

By typing "1," we specified a multiplication quiz. This simple program then types out:

$$\begin{array}{r} 12 \\ \times 23 \\ \hline = \ ? \end{array}$$

We must enter the answer (which we will leave as an exercise for the reader).

Let us summarize what we have learned thus far.

SUMMARY

We have now used most of the functions of a system:

—The *keyboard* is used to enter *commands* or *data*. Its *editing* capabilities are used to correct errors by moving the *cursor*.

—The *display* is used by the computer to communicate with us. It displays only characters (not pictures like a regular TV set).

—The *tape recorder* is used to store programs. It is inexpensive, but somewhat slow. The tape recorder is acceptable for use with games and short programs.

—The *microcomputer* has a special built-in program, the *monitor*, which is used to continually monitor the keyboard, and allow the user to use the system to process characters. The monitor also has a *file system* that allows it to retrieve symbolic *files* (programs — like "MATH") from the cassette.

The microcomputer is equipped with an *internal memory* , where it stores the program read from the cassette and the data typed at the keyboard.

In the next chapter, we will introduce all of the formal definitions, so that we can describe components and functions more accurately.

3

BASIC DEFINITIONS

MICROCOMPUTER APPLICATIONS

It is not possible to limit the number of applications for microcomputers. For the purpose of this book, however, it is convenient to classify microcomputer applications into three broad categories: personal applications, business applications, and industrial applications.

Personal applications of microcomputers are characterized by low cost systems, used in the home environment. These systems are meant to provide both entertainment and custom services for their users. Their technical characteristics are substantially different from microcomputers in the other two classes of applications.

Business microcomputers are used in the office environment. They are used for standardized business tasks such as payroll, inventory management, accounts payable and accounts receivable. The requirements of business microcomputers make them the most expensive microcomputer system of the three categories. This is due to their substantial processing requirements, and to the expensive terminals needed for satisfactory performance.

Industrial microcomputers are microcomputers installed in industrial applications for process control. Microcomputers incorporated into the home telephone system, at the hospital, in public buildings, elevators and cars fall into this category.

To differentiate between these applications, we will need to use a number of technical terms. This chapter will now present and define them.

Even the non-technical reader is strongly encouraged to read the definitions of these terms, if he or she wants to understand the reasons behind the comments and recommendations presented in the chapters that follow.

BASIC DEFINITIONS

A *microcomputer* is a computer in which a central processing unit is implemented with a single-chip microprocessor. In short, it is a computer which is implemented with LSI components.

LSI stands for Large Scale Integration. LSI is the result of the evolution of contemporary electronics towards microminiaturization of the components. Since the development of the discrete transistor (in the years that followed World War II), progress in the technology has allowed the implementation of an ever-increasing number of transistors on a single piece of silicon. The *chip* is the small rectangular piece of silicon, on which the circuit is realized. Circuits of up to 50,000 transistors can now be placed on such a chip. Technology has progressed from discrete transistors to SSI (Small Scale Integration), MSI (Medium Scale Integration), LSI and SLSI(Super Large Scale Integration — with densities of over 500,000 transistors per chip).

At this point, it is necessary to define the basic structure of the computer in order to describe the functional elements which constitute a microcomputer.

A *computer* can simply be defined as a general-purpose computing device capable of executing a *program*. A *program* is a sequence of instructions. Typical instructions manipulate information contained in a *memory* device. *Arithmetic instructions* perform operations such as addition, subtraction, or sometimes multiplication and division. *Logical instructions* perform logical operations such as a "logical AND" or a "logical OR." In addition, a *branch and test instruction* allows different portions of the program to be executed, depending upon the conditions being tested.

Every computer includes three basic functional elements:

1. *The Central Processing Unit* (CPU). The CPU is in charge of fetching the instructions from the memory, and executing them. It usually includes a very fast internal memory, called the *registers*, designed to increase the speed of instruction execution. Registers hold information for processing by the CPU.

2. *The Memory*. The memory is designed to store programs and the data on which they operate. A number of memory devices may be used, such as ROM, and RAM (described later in this chapter).

3. *Input-Output*. The input-output facilities allow the computer to communicate with the outside world. A typical input device is a keyboard through which data is entered into the system. A typical output device is a printer, or a CRT display, through which data

may be displayed or transmitted to the outside world.

The mechanical and electronic components of the system are known as *hardware*. The set of programs is called the *software*. An intermediate term is used for programs that reside in a special type of memory called *read-only memory* (ROM), which cannot be changed. They are called *firmware* since these programs (software) are implemented on a fixed hardware component.

In a microcomputer, the CPU is implemented as a single component, called the *microprocessor*.

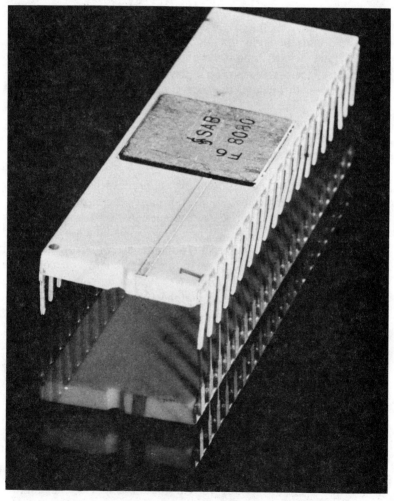

Figure 3-1: A microprocessor (8080). The package has 40 pins.

The word *chip* is now traditionally used to designate not only the rectangular piece of silicon bearing the circuit, but the component itself (called the "package").

Buses, which will be explained in more detail later, are simply communication paths for the system.

Bear in mind that all of these are simplified definitions. In fact, virtually all of the early microprocessors were only "almost complete" CPUs. As a result, they required a number of external circuits to form an actual CPU. Additional circuits, e.g., an external oscillator (the clock), a crystal (for precise time reference), and drivers (amplifiers) for the buses of the system were usually required (and often still are).

In addition to the three functional elements described previously — the CPU, the memory, and input-output facilities—a *microcomputer* traditionally includes the power supply necessary to provide the required voltages throughout the system, and a cabinet. If the memory of the system is small, a complete microcomputer system (excepting the power supply and the cabinet) can be implemented on a single board. However, in most general-purpose systems, it is desirable to allow for future expansion, such as the addition of more memory, or more external devices.

Complex external devices typically require specialized *interface boards,* or *controllers.* For this reason, most general-purpose microcomputers today have a similar appearance. A microcomputer today has the appearance of a small box (the actual dimensions depend on the manufacturer, but it is usually about the size of a drawer). Such a microcomputer box contains the basic CPU board, one or more memory boards, and one or more I/O boards designed to provide standard interfaces to common peripherals. It also includes the required power supply, and a cabinet.

Unlike traditional computers, many microcomputer boxes do not provide a front panel. A *front panel* is a panel equipped with lights and switches on the front of the box, designed for conveniently checking out programs at the hardware level. We will see later that such a facility is not a necessary item on a personal or a business computer system, and, since it adds substantially to the cost of the system, is not included.

Two standard *peripherals* are now provided with virtually every standard microcomputer. The standard *input* device is a keyboard, essentially analogous to a typewriter keyboard. Whenever the user presses a key on the keyboard, the character is encoded into a binary code (a set of 0's and 1's) and transmitted to the microcomputer.

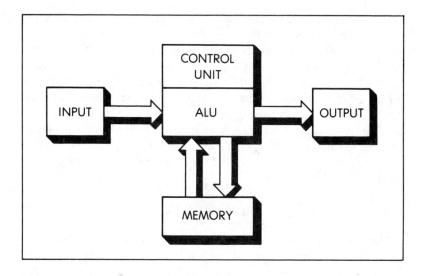

Figure 3-2: The five functional elements of every computer

The standard *output* device now provided with microcomputers is the CRT display. The CRT display is simply a TV monitor lacking the usual tuning and reception facilities. It is a screen designed to display characters generated by the microcomputer.

Since both the programs and data need to occupy a memory larger than the standard one provided in the microcomputer system, it is necessary to equip the microcomputer system with additional, cheaper, mass storage. Two alternatives are available. The most inexpensive is a tape cassette. An ordinary cassette recorder can be used to store programs, or data. Its major drawback is that it drastically limits the performance of the system.

The other alternative is the *floppy disk*, which will be described in detail later. The floppy disk has become the standard mass memory device for microcomputers. It is significantly more expensive than a tape cassette, but is the best mass storage medium available today, providing fast access to its contents at a reasonable cost.

We should note that at least two floppy disks are necessary for any practical application that manipulates files. In this way two files can be compared, or merged together, or one may be read while the other is being written. Such a facility is indispensable for convenient file processing. These concepts will be studied later in greater detail.

Depending upon the application considered, additional or different types of peripherals may be necessary. However, at this point we will assume that a standard microcomputer system consists of a microcomputer box (to implement the CPU and the memory, and the I/O interface), an input keyboard, a CRT display for output, and a dual disk drive (for mass storage). This is a "minimal configuration." In practice, a printer will also have to be added to the system. This standard configuration will be used as a reference point. A smaller system may be considered sufficient for specific personal uses or applications, while a larger system should be considered for more complex uses or applications.

MANUFACTURING A MICROPROCESSOR

How is a microprocessor manufactured? We have indicated that microprocessors are just one example of an LSI component. A typical LSI component is implemented on a *chip* bonded to a *dual in-line package* (a DIP). An illustration of a DIP appears in Figure 3-4. A DIP will typically have from 18 to 40 pins, through which the chip (inside the DIP) may communicate with the external world.

This technology is the result of an evolution of MOS. MOS stands for "metal oxide semiconductor." The semiconductor is *silicon*, which when injected (*doped*) with impurities (phosphorus or boron), becomes either positive or negative (technically it will have excess electrons or an electron deficiency, referred to as *holes*). The *oxide* is silicon oxide, used as an insulator on top of the silicon substrate. The *metal* is the gate of the transistor, which is implemented by depositing silicon or aluminum on top of the oxide.

The fabrication process is relatively simple in principle. A single crystal of silicon is grown with great care, resulting in a perfect crystalline lattice. This cylinder (four, five or six inches in diameter) is then cut into very thin slices (*wafers*). The wafers are polished, and look like circular mirrors. They are so thin that they are brittle, and can break like glass.

The chips are then created on the surface of these silicon wafers. From 100 to 500 chips measuring around 5 x 5 millimeters will usually be created. The transistors and other components are created on the chip by selectively diffusing impurities inside the silicon, depositing an oxide layer, and then depositing a metal layer on top of the oxide. A process of selective etching is used to define the areas where diffusion, oxidation or metalization is performed. This process, called

Figure 3-3: This system includes from left to right: the microcomputer box (opened), the disk, and the CRT terminal.

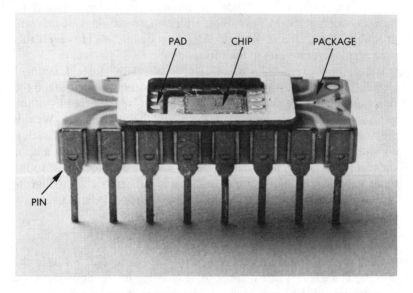

Figure 3-4: This DIP has been opened to show the chip

photolithography, is exactly analogous to printing pictures in a book. A mask is imprinted on top of the silicon wafer, and the photographic emulsion is exposed to light, developed and chemically etched. Diffusion, oxidation, and metalization will occur in the etched areas of the silicon. Once all the "chips" have been created on the wafer, the wafer will be *scribed* and broken into individual *chips*. Each of the chips is then mounted in individual packages, which will be sealed and become a DIP (technically, chips are called "dice" when still on the "wafer").

Other packages exist, but the most commonly used is the DIP (dual in-line package, such as the one in Figure 3-4).

After the *memory* chip, the *microprocessor* was one of the first standard LSI components to be introduced (in 1971). Since then, a large number of other LSI components have appeared, and virtually all the elements necessary to implement a complete microcomputer system are now available in LSI form. The very high number of transistors that can be implemented on a single chip has resulted in the implementation of a complete computer system on a single board. It has even become possible to implement a complete, though limited, computer in a single chip. This is the *one chip microcomputer.* However, one chip microcomputers are limited as to the amount of memory and the number of input-output lines they may have, and, for that reason, are exclusively utilized for control applications. They are not yet usable for personal or business computers. In the future, entire microcomputer boards will probably be reduced to a single-chip microcomputer. However, this time is still several years in the future.

Let us now examine in more detail each of the three functional elements of a microcomputer system. It is important to understand the function of these elements in order to comprehend the necessity of the various devices used to implement them, and their advantages. We will see that there are few "best solutions" independent of the application considered. Like most complex systems, (e.g., an appliance or a car), the computer system must be selected in view of the function of its intended application. For a choice to be made efficiently and intelligently, it is necessary to understand each of its functional elements.

THE CPU

CPU stands for Central Processing Unit. The CPU will fetch, decode, and execute instructions. It fetches the instructions from the memory where they are stored, and executes them by means of an arithmetic logical unit (ALU) in which arithmetic and logical operations are performed. The ALU is typically equipped with internal "registers" that provide high speed storage for frequently used data. Finally, instructions are decoded and internally sequenced by a special element in the CPU called the Control Unit (CU).

All of these functions are typically implemented on a single chip, the microprocessor chip. In practice, a number of support components that provide a stable reference frequency, such as the clock and its crystal, may be necessary on the board. Additional components are usually necessary to amplify the signals; they are the "drivers." Most microprocessors today are capable of processing 8 bits of data simultaneously ("bit" stands for "binary digit"—it is a logical "0" or "1"). An 8-bit microprocessor is a microprocessor that may process 8 bits (i.e., a byte) of data simultaneously. A *byte* is 8 bits.

THE BUSES

The microprocessor receives and transmits data to and from the outside world by means of eight lines, or the *data bus*. A bus is simply a set of lines, grouped by function. The data bus is said to be bidirectional, because data flows both to and from the microprocessor.

In order to indicate where the data comes from, or where it is going, an identification number that specifies the source or destination of the data must be provided by the microprocessor. This is called the *address*. Traditionally, a 16 line *address bus* is provided that allows a large number of locations (exactly 65,536) to be addressed. In computer jargon, one traditionally says "64K" instead of "65,536." One K represents $1,024 = 2^{10}$.

It should be briefly mentioned here that a data bus and an address bus are not yet sufficient for complete system operation. Because of the nature of the various electronic components in the system, it is necessary to provide *synchronization signals*. The signals for the orderly transfer of information along the data bus of the system are carried by the *control bus*. It is the third standard bus connected to the microprocessor. Let us leave buses for the time being, and look at the main hardware components of the system.

THE MEMORY

We have now seen that the memory of the system stores the programs and the data on which they operate. A memory is organized into *words*. In an 8-bit system, words are 8 bits wide. In this case, a word is just one byte long. In a 16-bit system, a word is 2 bytes long. In a 4-bit system, a word is 4 bits long (4 bits are called a "nibble"). A word does not always specify the same number of bits. A word is just the logical unit of information on which the processor will operate. In a traditional 8-bit system, a word happens to be equal to one byte.

An example of a byte stored in the memory of the system would be: "00000000" (eight zeroes). The programming section will demonstrate that all characters, all data, and all instructions in the system are represented by groups of 8 bits. Sometimes, more than one word must be used for a multi-word piece of information. However, it has not yet become practical to implement any other electronic system except the one based on the binary representation, i.e., whose logical states are always "0" or "1." For this reason, the binary system is universally used in digital computers.

Ideally, the complete memory of the system should be inexpensive, fast, and very large. Unfortunately, speed and size are not yet compatible with low cost. For this reason, two main types of memory are universally used: the *main memory* and the *auxiliary memory*, or "mass storage." The main memory of a system is contained in the microcomputer box, and is implemented in MOS LSI components.

The mass storage is typically a magnetic support such as a "floppy disk," or a magnetic cassette, which is relatively inexpensive, and offers a large storage capability. However, it is slower than main memory.

There are two essential types of components used for the implementation of the main memory. They are the Read Only Memory (ROM), and the Random Access Memory (RAM). Unfortunately, an MOS LSI memory (RAM) that can be both read and written is volatile, i.e., its contents disappear whenever power is removed. While this may be acceptable for temporary data, it is not acceptable for essential programs. For this reason, a permanent program must be stored in a different kind of memory, the ROM (Read Only Memory), which may not be written, but which is not volatile.

"10011!"

These two types of memories (ROM and RAM) are always required in a standard microcomputer system. In the case of personal and business systems, essential programs reside in ROM, and user programs reside in RAM, when executing. When not executing, user programs reside on a disk or a cassette.

We will see that the required memory size depends upon the application considered. A typical size might be 2K to 8K of ROM and at least 4K of RAM. These numbers will be discussed later.

INPUT-OUTPUT

The universal input device is the alphanumeric keyboard. The alphanumeric keyboard is simply the keyboard used in a typewriter (often equipped with additional keys), which allows the user to specify all the characters, numbers, and special symbols. The keyboard is normally equipped with a special *encoder,* which provides the 7- or 8-bit code directly to the microcomputer, every time that a key is pressed.

The keyboard has been found to be the most cost-efficient input medium for a human operator. Of course, in specialized environments, other input devices may be used. For example, in TV games, a joystick or other specialized buttons and switches may be used to play. They are cheaper and better suited to the environment but are limited in their information transmission capability.

The two universal output devices for a microcomputer have become the CRT display and the printer. Technically, it is not necessary to have both output devices. A printer, for example, is sufficient. However, a reliable printer is much more expensive than a CRT display, and has the disadvantage of being relatively slow when a lengthy text needs to be examined. A CRT display is therefore universally provided with every personal or business microcomputer system, in order to supply a fast, silent display of information. In most instances, a separate printer is necessary if permanent records are required.

Because input-output devices are generally complex mechanical or electronic devices, each device requires a separate *controller* (implemented as a board), which will receive the commands generated by the microcomputer or the status information from the device, and decode them. It will also read information from the device, and encode it in the format required for the microcomputer. In most cases, it is not possible to connect the microcomputer directly to a complex input-output device: *controller* or *interface boards* must be provided to connect them to the system.

A MICROPROCESSOR SYSTEM

A *microprocessor system* is essentially a complete board, without the power supply, the enclosure, and the peripherals. The so-called *architecture* of a "complete system" is shown in Figure 3-5. A microprocessor (which implements the function of the CPU) appears on the left. Shown on the right are the two types of memory, the ROM, and the RAM. The I/O interface, which communicates directly with the peripheral, is shown next on the right. The three wide horizontal paths are the three buses of the system. The I/O interface creates an *I/O bus,* which will connect directly to the peripherals. The clock and crystal, which appear on the far left, are usually external.

Several efforts at standardization have been made to provide an easy connection of external peripherals to the buses of a system. An example of this is the S-100 bus that has become important in the small computer market. This bus will be presented in a subsequent chapter.

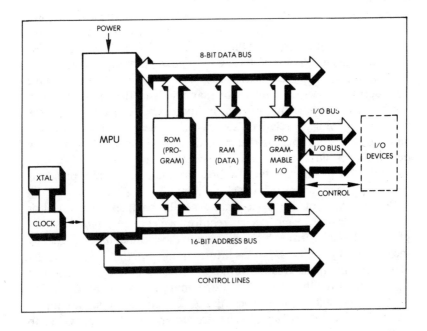

Figure 3-5:   Standard microprocessor system

THE MICROCOMPUTER SYSTEM

The microcomputer system is a complete, usable, microprocessor-based system. It includes all of the required functional elements: the microcomputer box (which contains one or more boards, plus power supply), a keyboard, a CRT display, and a printer.

Microcomputer or Minicomputer?

It has always been difficult to provide a good definition of what a minicomputer is. For most users, a minicomputer is a "computer box, equipped with at least 4K words of memory (typically 16 bits wide) and a Teletype (a standard typewriter-like input-output device), which sells for less that $10,000."

In practice, a minicomputer is a scaled-down version of the traditional large computer. Its processor is less powerful, but resides on one or two boards of logic, resulting in a much lower overall cost for the system. Because of their greatly reduced cost, minicomputers have been found to be very successful when used in a scientific environment and in limited business applications.

There is very little difference remaining between the minicomputer and the microcomputer. A microcomputer has been defined as a computer in which the CPU is implemented by a microprocessor chip, and is characterized by the fact that its components are LSI components (i.e., microminiaturized). Because of the difficulty in manufacturing highly complex CPUs on a single chip, the processing power of microprocessors has been limited until recently. However, because of their low cost, microcomputers have introduced a significant alternative to traditional minicomputers. Most users, in fact, have never needed the complete power of the minicomputer, but would have preferred a much lower price, which is exactly what the microcomputer brought. As a result, even minicomputer designs now generally incorporate a microprocessor. At least in the slowest versions of traditional minicomputers, microcomputers are used to implement the CPU. In other words, most slow minicomputers today are microcomputers. As the power of microprocessors steadily increases, we can predict that most minicomputers will eventually be microcomputers (and vice-versa). There is no longer a strict barrier between "micros" and "minis."

Differences still exist, however. A microcomputer is, generally, still a processor that has a rather weak (limited) instruction set and executes rather slowly (only on 8 bits at a time). Furthermore, its external com-

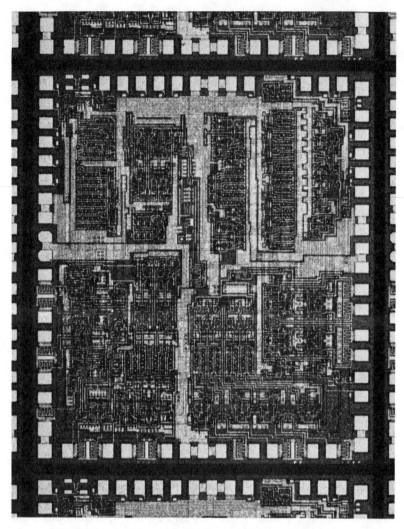

Figure 3-6: A "chip" on the wafer is surrounded by other chips

munication buses are restricted by the small number of pins of the microprocessor DIP (40 pins is typical).

In contrast, a minicomputer has a powerful instruction set and a wide bus so that it can transmit more signals simultaneously. (A typical word width for a minicomputer is 16 bits.) In short, a minicomputer executes faster and has more instructions than a microcomputer, with a word

Figure 3-7: A single-board microcomputer: the large chip at the center is the microprocessor

length twice as wide. A traditional minicomputer is still significantly faster than the *average* microcomputer.

Another important difference lies in the fact that minicomputers have existed for a greater number of years than microcomputers. As a result, the best-selling minicomputers are available with vast libraries of programs (software) that most microcomputers do not yet have.

However, the gap is now filling rapidly, thanks to the hobbyist market. For relatively powerful scientific applications, a fast minicomputer is still desirable. However, for the large number of new applications that do not require a significant processing power, the microcomputer is ideally suited.

Examples of minicomputers that have become microcomputers at the low end (the slowest) are: the Data General Nova (the Nova/2), and the LSI 11 (which implements in LSI the PDP 11/03).

Advantages of Microcomputers

The advantages of microcomputers are those of the LSI technology and of the single microprocessor chip. They include:

— Small size. A complete usable microcomputer can now be installed in a very small space. When the amount of memory and input-output functions can be limited, a complete microcomputer can even be implemented in a single chip. A complete system (one in which the processing power is comparable to a slow minicomputer) can now be easily implemented within the dimensions of an attache case. In fact, in some systems, when the space available is sufficient, the microcomputer itself resides within the enclosure of the keyboard. Microcomputers also use less power than minicomputers.

— Very low cost. The cost of a typical MOS chip is a few dollars. A complete system requires a small number of chips. The complete microcomputer box costs a few hundred dollars, depending upon the amount of memory it includes. Costs should continue to decrease.

— Reliability. A microcomputer uses few components and is, therefore, very reliable.

SUMMARY

All of the basic definitions of a microcomputer and its components have now been introduced. It is important to be familiar with these basic definitions in order to understand the material presented in the remaining chapters.

Because of the many mechanical and electronic options available today, every system differs as to the amount of memory, input-output facilities, and packaging. However, all of the systems presented in this book have the same "architecture," i.e., the same functional elements.

Evaluating these elements requires an understanding of their functions. For the more technically-minded reader, the next chapter will take a look inside the box (at the microcomputer system) to see how it works.

EXERCISES FOR SELF-TESTING

(Answers on Next Page)

Exercise 3.1:   *Which of the following elements normally reside in the microcomputer box:*
    1. CPU board   *4. special interface board*
    2. additional memory board   *5. power supply*
    3. disk controller board   *6. keyboard decoder*

Exercise 3.2:   *What is the difference between a minicomputer and a microcomputer?*

Exercise 3.3:   *Define a "bus."*

Exercise 3.4:   *What is the difference between a ROM and a RAM?*

Exercise 3.5:   *Does every system need a RAM?*

Exercise 3.6:   *Is a mass-storage indispensable?*

Exercise 3.7:   *What are the three functional elements of every computer system?*

Exercise 3.8:   *How many bits in a byte?*
    (1) 4, (2) 8, or (3) 16

Exercise 3.9:   *How many bits in a word?*
    (1) 4, (2) 8, or (3) 16

Exercise 3.10:   *What is an address?*

Exercise 3.11:   *Are the following data?*
    1. Characters
    2. Numbers

ANSWERS FOR SELF-TESTING EXERCISES

Exercise 3.1:   *1,2,3,4,5. The keyboard decoder is underneath the keyboard itself. Naturally, if the keyboard itself is integrated in the microcomputer box, then "6" is in the box also.*

Exercise 3.2:   *See text.*

Exercise 3.3:   *See text.*

Exercise 3.4:   *See text.*

Exercise 3.5:   *Yes, or else no input or output could occur, since the characters must be stored in RAM.*

Exercise 3.6:   *No, if the programs are short, and if the user is willing to retype them every time.*

Exercise 3.7:   *CPU, memory, input-output*

Exercise 3.8:   *8 bits*

Exercise 3.9:   *Undefined. This depends on the processor.*

Exercise 3.10:   *The address is a number which labels the location at which some data can be found.*

Exercise 3.11:   *1. Yes, 2. Yes.*

"The world has changed."

4

HOW THE SYSTEM WORKS

INTRODUCTION

The goal of this chapter is to explain the functions provided by the components of a microcomputer system in more detail. This technical information will be necessary for all those who wish to evaluate the capabilities and shortcomings of a system for a specific application.

This chapter provides the interested reader with an understanding of how a computer works internally, and what the various components do. It may be ignored by those who are not concerned with the technical operation of the system. Chapter 3 was a basic introduction. This chapter is a technical introduction.

THE BASIC ARCHITECTURE OF A SYSTEM

The three basic functional elements of any computer system are: the central processing unit (CPU), the memory, and the input-output.

Because it is not yet possible to implement a sufficient number of transistors into a single chip, each of these functions is presently performed by one or more hardware components (chips). These three functions and their implementation by specific components will now be examined in more detail.

The Central Processing Unit

The *central processing unit* (CPU) of the computer system fetches, decodes, and executes the instructions, which are contained in the *memory* of the system. A practical example will show how an instruction is fetched from the memory, brought into the CPU, decoded and executed.

For all practical purposes we will assume that the CPU is implemented by a microprocessor chip (commonly called MPU for microprocessor unit). This is not entirely correct: in most systems an external *crystal*, *clock*, and sometimes additional components may be required. However, this assumption will be sufficient for our example. Figure 4-1 shows the microprocessor on the left and the memory on the right.

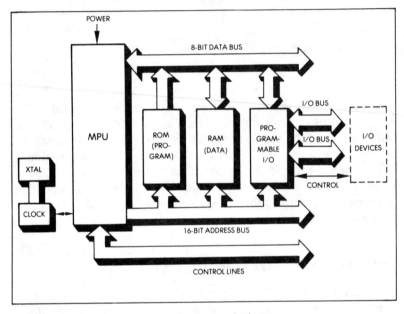

Figure 4-1:   The standard system

A *program* is executed instruction by instruction. Normally, each instruction is executed after the preceding one. These instructions are contained in the memory. In order to keep track of the location of an instruction within the memory, the *address* of the next instruction to be executed is contained in an internal register of the microprocessor called the program counter (PC).

A *register* is simply a small internal memory that can contain one or more words of information. In our example, to make things specific, we will assume that the *program counter* is a 16-bit register. In other words, this register can store 16 bits of binary information (0's and 1's). These 16 bits represent the binary address of the next instruction to be fetched from the memory. Fetching the next instruction from the memory should now be simple; the contents of the program counter will be gated out ("deposited") on the *address bus* of the microprocessor.

Our standard microprocessor is equipped with 16 pins called *address pins*, which allow the propagation of an address into the external world. 16 lines will carry this address to the memory chip. These 16 lines are the address bus of our microcomputer system.

Since a memory may usually either read or write, a *read signal* will generally be necessary. The microprocessor will generate the signal, and the memory will read the contents of the specified address. These contents, by definition, are the *instruction* that should be executed next by the microprocessor. A few hundred nanoseconds will elapse (a nanosecond is 10^{-9} seconds) before the data becomes physically available from the memory. This brief delay is called the *access time* of the memory. In a "standard" microcomputer system, the memory is 8 bits wide. In response to a 16-bit address, the memory will fetch a word that is only 8 bits wide. It is important to stress that there is no relationship between the number of bits supplied on the address bus and the number of bits that come out of the memory (8 bits in this example).

A similar example would be a street address. When given a street address, a person can find a house, or a building. The fact that the street address is small, or large, has no relation to the actual size of the building that will be found there. It might be a small house, or it might be a large apartment building. The data is totally unrelated to the address. The address is simply the location of the data within the structure. In our case the structure is the memory; in the example above, the structure is the city.

This 8-bit instruction must now be gated back to the microprocessor, so that it can be executed. All data in the system normally transits through a specialized bus, the *data bus*. The memory is equipped with 8 connections to the 8 lines of the data bus. The 8-bit instruction is therefore gated to the data bus and appears on the right of the illustration. The data travels along the data bus and to the left of the illustration towards the microprocessor. It is gated inside a special internal register of the microprocessor, called the *instruction register* (IR). This time, the register is 8 bits wide, as it must only contain 8 bits. This register is dedicated to holding the next instruction to be executed. When the time comes to execute this instruction, the 8 bits of this instruction will be decoded by the *decoder*, and the appropriate internal control signals will be automatically generated within the microprocessor, resulting in the execution of the instruction.

The mechanism for fetching and executing one instruction should now be clear. How will the next instruction be fetched? There is a special automatic mechanism: the program counter is equipped with an *incrementer* ("plus 1"). This incrementer increases the contents of the program counter by 1, every time that it is used. In this way, whenever the contents of the program counter are deposited on the address bus again, the next sequential address will be automatically accessed after the previous one. We have just built an *automatic sequencing mechanism* that will automatically fetch from successive memory locations.

There are, however, instances where the execution of a program must not be sequential. This is called a *branch* or *go to* instruction. In this case, the special *branch* instruction will explicitly modify the contents of the program counter in order to force a *jump* to a different location.

One question may still remain in the mind of the technically inclined reader: how is the instruction physically executed within the CPU? A brief description will be provided here.

Instruction fetch and decoding is performed by the *Control Unit* section of the CPU. Execution of the instruction is performed by the *ALU*

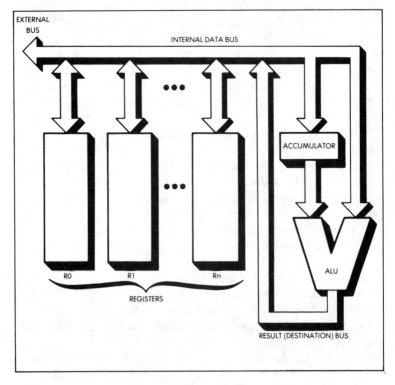

Figure 4-2: Inside the microprocessor

section of the CPU, which is normally equipped with specialized *internal registers*. An illustration of a typical ALU appears in Figure 4-2. The vertical rectangles on the left of the illustration are the *registers*. In the case of our "standard" microprocessor, these registers contain 8 bits. The V-shaped symbol on the right of the illustration is the *arithmetic logical unit* (ALU). The ALU is in charge of actually performing the arithmetic and logical operations specified by the instruction. In addition, ALUs are typically equipped with a *shifter* that may *shift* the result left or right by one or more bit positions. Attached to the ALU is a special register called the *status* or *flags* register, which contains *flags*. A *flag* is a special bit which memorizes an internal condition. Such special conditions are an arithmetic carry, a zero result, a negative result, or other special events. Special instructions within the program may test these conditions and cause branches in the function of specified events.

In order to illustrate the way the CPU operates, let us execute a simple addition of the contents of two internal registers. We will assume that registers R0 and R1 have each been loaded by specific instructions with 8-bit data. Each register contains 8 binary bits. Our goal now is to add the contents of R0 and R1, and deposit the results into R0. At the

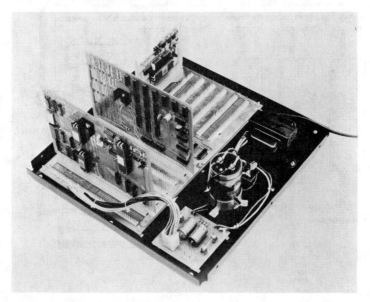

Figure 4-3: Inside the microcomputer box (a SWTPC 6800): the three boards on the left are the CPU, the memory, and the I/O interface. The power supply is on the right.

end of the operation, the contents of R1 should be intact, and R0 should contain the sum of the two numbers. The *addition* instruction will do exactly this. The contents of R0 will be gated towards the top of the illustration, and towards the right input of the ALU. Next, the contents of R1 will be gated along the same internal data bus towards the left input of the ALU. Then an addition order will be transmitted by the control unit to the ALU. The ALU will add, then place the result of the addition on its output lines towards the bottom of the illustration, on the right. This sum will finally be gated to the destination register, R0 in our example. Reading from a register does not change its contents. The contents of R1 will, therefore, not be affected by the addition operation. However, since the sum has been written into R0, R0 will contain the sum of the two numbers at the end of the operation; its original contents will have been erased. Note that, as a result of the addition, one or more of the flags will be automatically set by the ALU (in particular: carry, zero, sign).

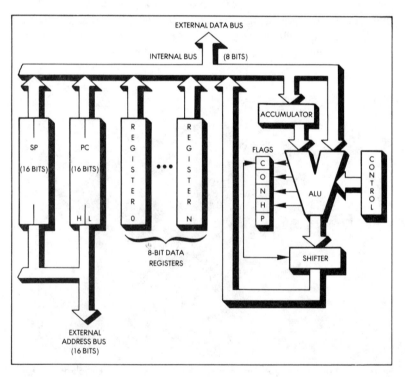

Figure 4-4:   This detailed diagram shows the flags, the shifter, and the PC.

Let us now summarize the operation of a CPU: the Control Unit fetches an instruction from the memory, brings it into the instruction register, decodes it and then generates the proper control signals automatically.

The ALU is in charge of executing the specified operation, either on the internal registers of the MPU, or sometimes directly on the data supplied from the external world via the data bus. Such data might be supplied from the *memory,* or from an *input-output device.*

The time has now come to take a look at the outside world: the memory and input-output.

The Memory

We have seen that the memory stores the program. The memory must also store *data* that the user has entered, or that is created during program execution. Recall that MOS memory (memory using integrated circuits) has one significant drawback today: read/write memories (i.e., memories where information can be both written and read) are volatile. This means that their contents disappear when power is no longer applied. For this reason, two types of memories are used in microcomputer systems: ROMs and RAMs. In older systems, like minicomputers, this problem did not exist. *Core* technology was used to implement memories. Each bit of information (i.e., a logical "0" or "1") was stored in a ferrite torus, analogous in shape to a doughnut. Since the core was always magnetized in one direction or another, this memory did not require power to retain information. In view of the utilization of the MOS technology, it is now necessary to use two types of memory in the system.

The first type of memory is *RAM* (or Random Access Memory). RAM is a memory that can be both read and written. RAM must be used in a system for data, otherwise it would not be possible for the MPU to store the results of its computations or the data that it might be reading from the keyboard or another input device. The size of a program, or file, which you wish to load in a microcomputer system is limited by the amount of RAM the system has. The next section describes the two types of technologies used to implement RAM: static and dynamic memories.

The second type is *ROM* (or Read Only Memory). ROM is non-volatile, and is used to store programs. Once the information has been deposited in a ROM, it can (in principle) no longer be changed. Provided that a program is correct, it will no longer need to be changed, and can, therefore, reside in ROM. This is the case in most industrial applications. In particular, the "monitor" program of your microcomputer is normally in ROM, as there is no need to change it. However, most users who develop a program by themselves require the capability of changing it. For this reason, alternative types of ROMs are available, called *PROMs* or *RPROMs*. Although abbreviations may vary, a PROM is a user Programmable Read Only Memory. It uses a fusible link technology, which allows the user to deposit 0's and 1's in it, using a relatively low-cost PROM programmer. PROMs are inexpensive. However, because they use fusible link technology, once "programmed," they can no longer be changed. They are still not entirely adequate for our purposes. The type most frequently used is the RPROM or EPROM. These abbreviations stand for Reprogrammable PROM, or Ultraviolet Erasable PROM, or Electrically Erasable PROM. With this type of memory, the user may "program" the chip, execute the program, and then later erase the contents and reprogram. This type of memory is normally used in any fixed-program development, i.e., in industrial applications.

Personal and business applications differ from industrial applications. In personal and business applications, a variety of programs that must reside in succession in the memory of the system must be executed throughout the day. For this reason, ROMs, PROMs, or EPROMs are

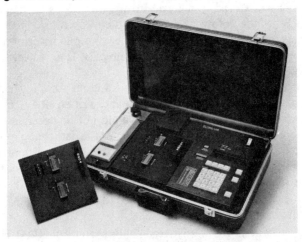

Figure 4-5: PROM programmer in attache case format. Sockets are for inserting the PROMs. The bit pattern is entered via the hexadecimal keyboard.

used less in such systems (except for the monitor program). EPROMs are intended for use with fixed programs that permanently reside in the system, such as the "monitor" program on the personal or business system. However, the user programs on such systems will always reside in RAM. The user must be aware that every time he or she turns the power off, his or her program will disappear. This is why every system must be equipped with an auxiliary *mass memory*, such as a floppy disk, on which the programs can be permanently recorded. Every time that the user wishes to execute a program, the program must be copied from the disk into the system. This is a simple, fast operation that may even be done automatically if the system has a good *disk operating system* (DOS). The operation is then invisible to the user.

Static and Dynamic RAMs

The details of the technology should not concern the user here. Simply, for systems intended to have a small memory, static RAM is usually utilized, as it results in a less expensive board. In larger systems, let us say more than 16K bytes, dynamic RAM is usually used. For all practical purposes, hobbyists and business systems would seldom use less than 16K of memory, and therefore most memory boards would be dynamic. Provided that the price is right, a static RAM board can be used with no technical impact on the system. This topic will therefore not be discussed further here.

The Input-Output

Typical input-output devices in a microcomputer system consist of the *keyboard* for input, and a *CRT display* for output. Many other devices may also be used. These devices usually provide or require 8-bit parallel data. In other words, a typical keyboard will put 8 bits on a bus that correspond to the code of the character which was pressed. Similarly, when the character is sent to the CRT display, it is sent as 8 bits parallel.

Other input-output devices prefer a *serial communications* scheme. A *Teletype* is one of them. The *Teletype* is a popular "teletypewriter" with a typewriter-like keyboard and printing mechanism. When a key is pressed on the Teletype, a succession of 11 bits is sent towards the microcomputer system. The first bit is called the "start" bit. It is followed by 8 data bits, which encode the character. The message is terminated by two "stop" bits. As usual, 8 bits carry the information representing the character to the microcomputer. However, this time

INPUT

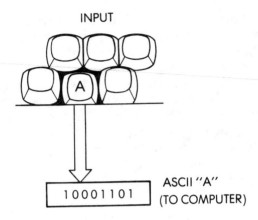

```
1 0 0 0 1 1 0 1
```

ASCII "A"
(TO COMPUTER)

Figure 4-6: Pressing a key on the keyboard generates an 8-bit code which is transmitted here in parallel.

they are transmitted *serially*, i.e., one after the other on a single wire.

In summary, there are *serial* and *parallel* input-output devices. Two types of interface chips have been created in order to easily interface with the microcomputer data bus. In addition to these two basic chips, which will be described briefly here, more complex input-output devices require more complex *interface logic*, i.e., an *interface board*. Input-output devices also occasionally require that an 8-bit code sent from the microcomputer system to the device be interpreted as a command, rather than as simple data. In this case, a *command decoder* must be provided; this is a *controller board*. A controller board receives 8-bit commands, and then decodes and translates them into a sequence of steps that will carry out the specified command. *Controllers* are

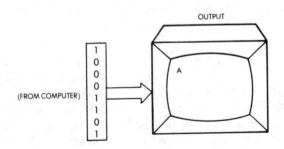

Figure 4-7: The binary code for A is sent to the CRT display

typically required for intelligent CRT displays and disk drive units.

The two basic chips used in a microcomputer system to provide serial and parallel interface are, respectively, the *UART* and the *PIO*. Abbreviations for a PIO vary with the manufacturer. For purposes of simplicity, the letters PIO will be used here.

UART stands for "Universal Asynchronous Receiver Transmitter." The details of its operation need not concern us here. A diagram of a UART appears in Figure 4-8. The role of a UART is to convert parallel into serial, and serial into parallel. A UART will accept an 8-bit parallel input, and convert it into a sequence of 8 bits (or more) on a serial line. It may simultaneously receive serial input signals and convert them into an 8-bit parallel output. The 8-bit parallel input and the 8-bit parallel output are normally connected to the bidirectional data bus of the microprocessor. The serial input and the serial output of the UART are connected to specific devices.

The PIO stands for "Parallel Programmable Input-Output." It connects to the microprocessor data bus, and creates two or more I/O *ports* (I/O stands for "input-output"). A *port* is simply an 8-bit connection (in this case) to the outside world. Out of a single 8-bit connection to the data bus it creates two or more connections to the outside world. It also provides *internal buffering*: each I/O port is equipped with an 8-bit register, a "buffer," that memorizes information. In addition, a PIO is programmable, and can manage I/O control protocols. This is called *handshaking*. The PIO and the UART are the universal chips found on most microcomputer boards that provide easy interface to either serial or parallel devices. Again, additional logic may be needed if the re-

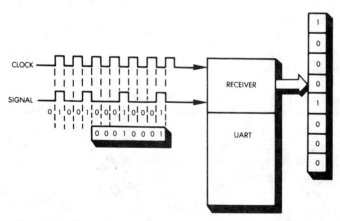

Figure 4-8:   The UART converts serial to parallel, and parallel to serial

quired function does not simply transmit characters, but is also used to transmit commands or status information: such information may need to be decoded and executed by its own control board. In such a case, a *controller board* is also required.

All of the basic chips of a microcomputer system have now been described. Additional special-purpose chips can perform other functions. In particular, device control functions are facilitated by one-chip device controllers, such as the FDC or "floppy disk controller," or the CRTC or "CRT controller." Single-chip analog-to-digital converters also exist.

The Power Supply

The power supply provides a regulated (stable) voltage (or voltages) to the circuits. It is an important element, both in terms of cost and system reliability. The power supply is also an important physical factor, as it often occupies one-fifth of the volume of the microcomputer box.

The four functional elements of a power supply appear in Figure 4-9.

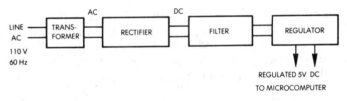

Figure 4-9:   The four elements of a power supply

SUMMARY

The three functional elements of a microcomputer system, the CPU, the memory, and the input-output devices, were described in this chapter. Each of these functions can be performed by specialized LSI chips, which can be mounted on one or more boards to form the microcomputer boards. The internal execution of an instruction within the CPU was also described.

We are now ready to use the system by either writing a program or installing a program in the memory of the system in order to execute the requested function. Let us examine what programming involves.

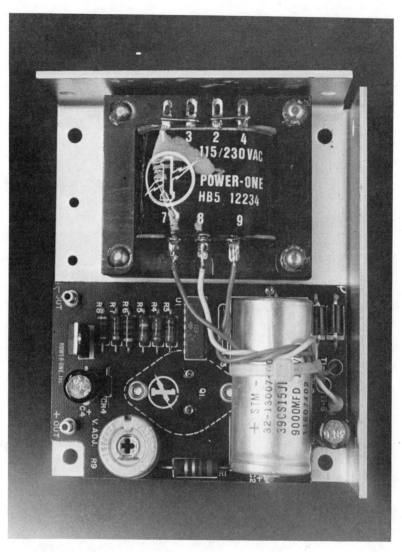

Figure 4-10:   Microcomputer power supply shows its functional elements ("Power-One")

"I did not make a programming error!"

5

PROGRAMMING THE COMPUTER

BASIC DEFINITIONS

A *program* is a sequence of orders, or *instructions,* to a computer that will solve a specific problem. In the field of business applications this is called Electronic Data Processing, or EDP, where the main function of a program is to process files containing data.

In the personal computing environment, programs can be much more varied. They may play games, control an alarm system within a house, or provide word processing capabilities.

Ideally, it would be desirable to tell a computer what to do in plain English. Unfortunately, it has been proven that a so-called "natural language" (English or another language) cannot be used to communicate with a computer, as it is ambiguous. Only a small subset of a natural language can be used to specify orders to a computer. In addition, the necessity of efficient processing requires that instructions be of a well-defined length. For this reason, *programming languages* have been created that are efficient tools (from the computer's standpoint) for executing programs. Their efficiency at the user level will be evaluated later in this chapter. The only "language" that any computer actually understands consists of sequences of 0's and 1's, i.e., instructions expressed in the *binary* system. This is called *machine language.*

Once a problem has been defined, its solution will be specified as an *algorithm.* The algorithm is simply a step-by-step specification of the solution to the problem. As an example, here is a simplified traffic control algorithm for a typical intersection:
— Turn green on for direction A.
— Wait two minutes.
— Switch green off.
— Turn amber on for direction A.

— Wait thirty seconds.
— Turn amber off.
— Turn red on.
— Turn green on for direction B.
— Wait one minute.
— Turn amber on for direction B.
— Wait twenty seconds.
— Turn red on for direction B.
— Go back to the first step.

The above *algorithm*, or solution to a problem, is also an example of a "fixed cycle loop." It is a "loop" because after the last step of the algorithm is executed, the first step is repeated. Control in a loop goes around from the last to the first step.

Note that in addition to being a loop, its cycle is "fixed" according to a set time sequence. With the use of a microcomputer, the algorithm could be improved to provide a more dynamic response at the intersection, that is, it could provide a light pattern that would change as the traffic conditions change (e.g., during different hours of the day or days of the week).

Translating an algorithm into a computer language is called *programming*. Programming can be done in essentially two ways:

1. In machine-level language. Programming in machine-level language involves specifying instructions that the computer can immediately or readily execute. Because it is tedious and error-prone to program directly in binary (using 0's and 1's), a symbolic representation of instructions is used. This is called *assembly-level language*. For example, the instruction:

"ADD R0, R1"

means "add the contents of registers R0 and R1 and deposit the results into R0." This instruction is expressed in *symbolic form*. It must be translated into binary bits in order to be executed by the microcomputer. This translation is performed by a special program called the *assembler*.

The assembler is simply an automatic translation program that accepts an assembly-level program, and then translates it into the machine code or binary code for the microprocessor. It translates each symbolic instruction into one binary instruction. These binary instructions (typically 8, 16 or 24 bits long) can then be placed in the memory of the system and executed.

Entering a program into the memory of the system can be done directly, in the case of a ROM (by inserting a component), or via a peripheral. In a typical system, the program is typed on the keyboard, transferred into RAM memory, and then stored in a mass memory such as the disk. When the program is used, it is loaded from the disk into the RAM memory of the system, where it can be executed or translated.

2. In high-level language. The second option is to write a program in a higher-level language. A high-level language is a language closer to spoken English, and much easier for the user to program in. Statements or instructions in high-level language are usually fairly easy to understand, but still obey a rigid syntax, so that any ambiguities are eliminated. There are several high-level languages available. However, for business and personal purposes, there is only one major high-level language universally used for microprocessors today: this is the language called BASIC. Programming in BASIC will be described in a later chapter. Another language popular in industrial and control applications of microprocessors is PL/M (Programming Language for Microprocessors), initially developed by Intel (and trademarked by Intel). One of the important differences between PL/M and BASIC is that PL/M is a *compiler*, while BASIC is an *interpreter*. Let us discuss this in more detail. Other languages will be described in Chapter 6.

An *interpreter* is the special program required to interpret and execute a higher-level language such as BASIC. Of course, the instructions in the BASIC language must eventually be converted into the binary format, which is the only language the microcomputer can execute. Two options are available. Either each statement may be translated into machine code in sequence, thus creating an *object code* which can then be executed separately, or each line of the high-level language may be translated, and then executed immediately before looking at the next line. When each line is immediately translated and executed, it is an interpreter program. When the entire program is translated into object code, ready for later execution, it is a compiler.

The advantage of an interpreter is that every time a line is typed it can be executed without any delay. Lines may be changed freely in the program without incurring any delay for execution. This is a great convenience for efficient programming. The disadvantage of the interpreter is that most programs include a large number of loops. Whenever a loop is executed repeatedly, each statement is translated over and over again. When a compiler is used, each line is translated only once and then execution is performed with high efficiency on the machine code representation. Why then is an interpreter so popular? Let us look at the compiler.

A compiler translates the entire program into machine code. Then, after a substantial delay for the translation of the complete program, execution may proceed. If any one line in the program is to be changed, usually the complete program must be recompiled, causing a significant delay. For this reason, interpreters are most popular for program development, as they allow direct interaction within the system. Interpreters are said to be interactive: a statement may be executed, changed, and then executed again. In order to remedy the intrinsically lower performance of interpreters, *compiler versions* of BASIC are also available. Once a program has been completely debugged and is ready to execute with no further changes, a BASIC compiler will translate the source program into its machine code representation, which will be executed from then on.

It is important to note here that many users find that the advantages of fast and convenient program development inherent in the interpreter far outweigh the loss in efficiency. This would not be true, however, in a control environment where most users would consider using a compiler such as PL/M, or direct coding in assembly-level language.

PROGRAMMING LANGUAGES

A large number of programming languages have been invented. Each offers specific advantages to some class of users. Remember, however, that the main criterion for judging a high-level programming language is usually by its convenience to a specific class of users. For some users, convenience means ease of programming in a specific language. For other users, it means the availability of programs in this language that can readily be used.

Because PL/M was the first compiler developed for microprocessors, it is widely accepted. Several versions of FORTRAN have now become available. FORTRAN is an old and respectable compiler. PASCAL is also becoming increasingly available.

For all practical purposes, the *interpreter* most widely used at this time is BASIC.

FLOW CHARTING

Flow charting is crucial to successful programming. A flowchart is simply the symbolic representation of the algorithm to be executed. Within a flowchart, two basic symbols are used, with some variations: rectangles and diamonds.

A *rectangle* is used for orders or "statements," such as "open the door" or "A = 2."

A *diamond* is used for a test such as "if it boils, then add chemical C," or "if A = 2, then go to point 51 of the flowchart," or "if X = 1, print ERROR."

Let us consider an example. The following is a "thermostat algorithm."

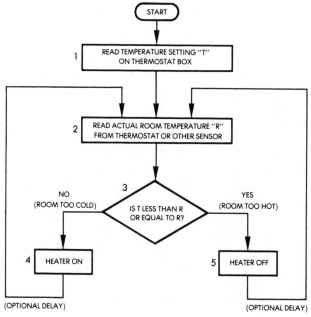

Figure 5-1: The flowchart represents the algorithm

— In step "1", the temperature, "T," set manually on the thermostat box is read.

— In step "2," the actual room temperature, "R," is measured with an appropriate device.

— In steps "3," "4," and "5," the following occurs:

— If the room is too hot "R > T," (read "R greater than T"), then turn the heater off.

— If the room is too cold, turn it on.

The diamond-shaped symbol is used in "3" as a test occurs. Two arrows come out of the diamond, depending upon the two possible outcomes of the test. Note that there could be more than two.

Once an algorithm has been flow charted, it becomes a much simpler matter to program it. The following is the highly recommended method for writing programs that work:

1. Develop the correct algorithm that specifies the solution to the problem.
2. Make a flowchart of the algorithm.
3. Program the algorithm in the language of your choice.

Experience indicates that approximately 10% of the population can program directly from the algorithm into the programming language, and produce a correct program. Unfortunately, experience also indicates that 90% of the population believes that it belongs to this 10%!

In short, most people do not believe that it is necessary to develop a flowchart until their program does not work. The odds are overwhelmingly against you if you do not flow chart.

However, experience also indicates that 90% of the population does not believe this until their programs fail. Let us, therefore, not discuss this subject further.

Note that flow charting is easy: there is no convention or requirement as to what is written in a "box." You may use the English language, your own abbreviations, or even a programming language.

A flowchart diagram illustrates the "flow" of execution in time, hence its name: "flowchart."

Special symbols are sometimes used to "clarify" the flowchart, for example, special symbols for punched cards, disks, or tape printouts.

INFORMATION REPRESENTATION IN A MICROCOMPUTER

Electronic switching circuits are characterized by either a "0" or a "1" state. All electronic computers must therefore represent information stored within the system in binary form, i.e., as "0's" or "1's". The binary system represents all numbers as sequences of zeroes and ones. For all practical purposes, an 8-bit microprocessor stores and manipulates information that is 8 bits wide (this is called a "byte"). All *data* and *instructions* are normally encoded as one or more bytes. Typical microcomputer instructions, for example, are either one byte, two bytes, or three bytes long. Characters are universally encoded as one byte; 8 bits allow 2^8 combinations, or 256 different codes, or 256 different characters. (If "parity" is implemented, only 7 bits are available, which would allow 2^7, or 128 combinations.) As an example of character representation, the ASCII table appears in Figure 5-2.

The representation of large integers requires two or more bytes. Two bytes or 16 bits only allow up to 64K, or 65,536 combinations (1K = 1,024). This is still not sufficient in most cases, therefore 3 bytes or more must be used just for integers. Special conventions are used for decimal

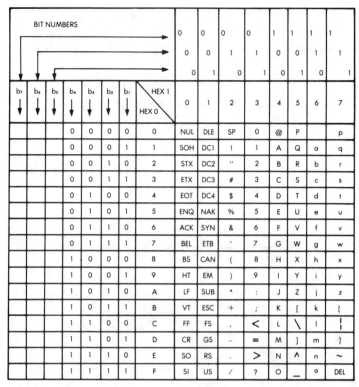

Figure 5-2: ASCII table

b7	b6	b5	b4	b3	b2	b1	HEX	0	1	2	3	4	5	6	7
			0	0	0	0	0	NUL	DLE	SP	0	@	P		p
			0	0	0	1	1	SOH	DC1	!	1	A	Q	a	q
			0	0	1	0	2	STX	DC2	"	2	B	R	b	r
			0	0	1	1	3	ETX	DC3	#	3	C	S	c	s
			0	1	0	0	4	EOT	DC4	$	4	D	T	d	t
			0	1	0	1	5	ENQ	NAK	%	5	E	U	e	u
			0	1	1	0	6	ACK	SYN	&	6	F	V	f	v
			0	1	1	1	7	BEL	ETB	'	7	G	W	g	w
			1	0	0	0	8	BS	CAN	(	8	H	X	h	x
			1	0	0	1	9	HT	EM	)	9	I	Y	i	y
			1	0	1	0	A	LF	SUB	*	:	J	Z	j	z
			1	0	1	1	B	VT	ESC	+	;	K	[	k	{
			1	1	0	0	C	FF	FS	,	<	L	\	l	|
			1	1	0	1	D	CR	GS	-	=	M	]	m	}
			1	1	1	0	E	SO	RS	.	>	N	^	n	~
			1	1	1	1	F	SI	US	/	?	O	_	o	DEL

ACK	Acknowledge	FF	Form feed
BEL	Bell	FS	Form separator
BS	Backspace	GS	Group separator
CAN	Cancel	HT	Horizontal tab
CR	Carriage return	LF	Line feed
DC1	Direct control 1	NAK	Negative acknowledge
DC2	Direct control 2	NUL	Null
DC3	Direct control 3	RS	Record separator
DC4	Direct control 4	SI	Shift in
DEL	Delete	SO	Shift out
DLE	Data link escape	SOH	Start of heading
EM	End of medium	SP	Space
ENQ	Enquiry	STX	Start text
EOT	End of transmission	SUB	Substitute
ESC	Escape	SYN	Synchronous idle
ETB	End transmission block	US	Unit separator
ETX	End text	VT	Vertical tab

Figure 5-3: Abbreviations of ASCII code table

numbers; this is called "floating-point representation." As an example, the binary representation of the integers 0 through 7 appears below. Three bits are necessary to represent eight possible combinations.

INTEGER	BINARY REPRESENTATION
0	000
1	001
2	010
3	011
4	100
5	101
6	110
7	111

LOGICAL OPERATIONS

Binary arithmetic on binary numbers is quite straightforward, at least in the case of integers:

$0 + 0 = 0$

$0 + 1 = 1$

$1 + 0 = 1$

$1 + 1 = 10$ (or 0, with a carry of 1)

The four main logical operations that can be performed on binary numbers are: OR, AND, XOR, and NOT. OR is represented by a V-shaped symbol, and AND is represented by an inverted V symbol: $\wedge$.

Each operation can be defined by its *truth-table*. A truth-table is simply a listing of results when the operation is applied to each of the variables. Four truth-tables for (OR, AND, XOR, and NOT) appear below.

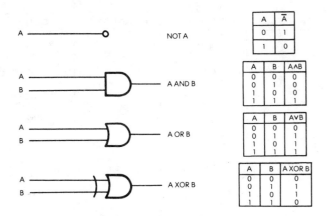

Figure 5-4:   The basic truth-tables

EXTERNAL REPRESENTATION

Information must be represented externally. Usually, it is represented *symbolically,* with alphanumeric symbols and decimal numbers. Whenever the required facilities are not available to convert the binary number to its alphanumeric representation, *hexadecimal* is used.

The *hexadecimal* representation is simply a way to encode four binary bits (a "nibble") into one symbol. Four bits may generate up to 16 combinations ("hex" means 6 in Greek). Therefore, the ten symbols from 0 through 9 are used, and the next six symbols are simply the letters A through F. In this way, an 8-bit byte may be represented by two hexadecimal symbols. The conversion table from binary to hexadecimal appears in Figure 5-5.

As an example, FF in hexadecimal stands for "1111 1111" in binary. Hexadecimal is convenient, as it is much easier to memorize, or to handle, than binary. In addition, hexadecimal may be conveniently and economically displayed on light emitting diodes or input through a 16 key keyboard. On the most inexpensive microcomputer boards, all input as well as output is hexadecimal.

The 8 digits from 0 to 7 can be used to represent any combination of 3 binary bits. This is the *octal* representation.

Octal has been used extensively with minicomputers. It is relatively inefficient, and can be considered a thing of the past, despite the insistence of some manufacturers on providing octal, rather than hexadecimal. However, this is a minor point.

DECIMAL	BINARY	HEXADECIMAL	OCTAL
0	0000	0	00
1	0001	1	01
2	0010	2	02
3	0011	3	03
4	0100	4	04
5	0101	5	05
6	0110	6	06
7	0111	7	07
8	1000	8	10
9	1001	9	11
10	1010	A	12
11	1011	B	13
12	1100	C	14
13	1101	D	15
14	1110	E	16
15	1111	F	17

Figure 5-5: Hexadecimal-octal conversion table

DEVELOPING A PROGRAM

The first step toward developing a program is to draw a flowchart. A program is then written on paper in the language selected, either in assembly-level or high-level language. The program is input through a keyboard into the main memory of the system (the RAM). Errors will nearly always be made during the input phase of this program. For this reason, it is not only important, but virtually indispensable, to have a convenient way to enter corrections, move text, make insertions, deletions, or look for a specified pattern.

This is the function of the *editor* program. The editor is a standard program available on any system, designed to facilitate the entry of the data or the program. Because the editor will never be changed by the user, it often resides in ROM. On some systems, in order to free additional memory space, the editor may reside on external storage such as a disk file, and have to be loaded into the central memory of the system prior to its use.

After being typed in, and after typing errors are corrected, the user program resides in symbolic form in the central memory of the system. At this point, the program is a string (a sequence of characters and numbers) typically encoded in the ASCII format described previously. Assuming that the program was written in assembly-level language, it must be translated from its symbolic representation into *object-code* so that the microcomputer can execute. The *assembler* program is now loaded from a disk file into the central memory of the system (the RAM). The user invokes the assembler to translate the *symbolic* program into the object-code. The assembler performs this translation automatically, and generates diagnostics if it detects any syntax errors. Assuming that the assembly has been successful (no syntactic errors were found by the assembler), the object-code is now ready to execute. Often, the object-code may have to be loaded at a different place in the memory than the one it was originally intended for. In this case, a *loader* program is required to place the program at the appropriate memory location and to update all the addresses it contains. We will now assume that the object-code resides in the memory of the system and is ready to execute. Because most programs never execute correctly the first time, if we should simply go ahead and execute this object-code, the odds are that the execution would be incorrect. Unfortunately, there would be virtually no obvious way to detect what went wrong, as nothing visible would happen.

In order to determine what has gone wrong, and where, a *debugger* program is necessary. Debugging refers to the tracing and removal of errors from a program. A debugger oversees the following functions: it automatically stops execution of a program at selected locations (breakpoints), and it examines or modifies the register or memory contents.

Prior to running the program, the user sets *breakpoints*: they are simply addresses at which the debugger will automatically stop the program execution. The program then executes under the control of the debugger. Whenever one of the breakpoints is reached, the debugger stops execution. The user may then examine the registers and memory, and make sure that the results are correct. If the results are not correct, then the segment of the program that caused the error can be isolated. This error diagnostic can be refined by setting additional breakpoints, as needed. Usually, many errors are found, and the user must type in corrections. The entire procedure just described must then be performed again until the program is "completely debugged," and executes successfully, that is, it is "correct" (or rather presumed correct). In practice, errors are almost always found later, in any large program. However, the program can at this point be considered correct enough for execution in the intended environment.

Guarding against all possible situations that might trigger incorrect behavior is virtually impossible in a long program. A long program may prove perfectly reliable, and always execute correctly. Hidden errors in the program may only come to light when an unusual combination of events occurs, such as when another user attempts to use this program for another purpose. These errors are usually mild, and do not cause the system to misbehave significantly (they are called "soft errors").

Another reason a long program may not execute correctly is the actual complexity of the system. Some systems are so complex that the odds of hidden bugs triggering a system failure are high.

Fortunately, however, most user programs never reach this level of complexity. They can, therefore, be deemed correct for all practical purposes, i.e., they will be more correct and reliable than most complex mechanical devices (such as a car, for example).

REQUIRED SOFTWARE FOR PROGRAM DEVELOPMENT

It has been seen that the minimum software required for program development consists of an *editor*, an *assembler*, an *interpreter* or a *compiler* (if a high level language is used), and a *debugger*. Every reasonable system provides these facilities. In addition, if disk storage is going to be used, a *disk operating system* (DOS) must be available. A DOS is the program (supplied by the manufacturer) that automates disk usage. In addition, the power of disk operating systems varies greatly, depending upon the manufacturer. Ideally, using a DOS should make it possible to manipulate files symbolically and not have to worry about their actual physical allocation. The system should take care of all required housekeeping and perform all transfers automatically. Unfortunately, this is not always the case. This will be discussed in the disk section in Chapter 9.

If an interactive language such as BASIC is going to be used, then an *interpreter* must be available for that language. Finally, additional facilities such as a *simulator* or an *emulator*, must be available for specific hardware developments.

Finally, we should mention the *monitor* program. Every microcomputer comes equipped with a ROM-resident monitor, or else it could not be used: there would be no way to type a command at the keyboard, since the microprocessor does nothing until it starts executing a program. Whenever the system is started, a "Reset" is performed. The microprocessor then starts executing a program that resides at a specific memory location (let us say address 0, for example). This program may clear the registers, even verify that everything is functioning properly by running some diagnostics, then start monitoring the keyboard, and do nothing else. The user will hit a key on the keyboard, and the monitor program will pick up the character and process it.

The "monitor" often includes a number of debugging facilities, such as hexadecimal/octal/binary conversion and facilities to examine and change registers or memory.

SO YOU WANT TO PROGRAM?

When programming your computer, you have two possible options:
— If you just want to use the microcomputer and are not concerned about what happens inside, then there is no reason to use assembly-level instructions, which manipulate registers. You will be using a high-level language, such as BASIC. To learn how, read the next chapter.

— The second possibility is to program in assembly language or even in hexadecimal. If you choose hexadecimal, and have a limited budget, then all you need is a microcomputer board and a power supply. The board should have a keyboard for entering instructions or data, and an LED display, preferably with six LEDs, so that both an address and the data at that address may be displayed simultaneously (in hexadecimal). In addition, it is a great convenience to have a cassette recorder interface directly on the board, so that programs can be saved for later use, rather than retyped.

A minimal personal computer, with a full keyboard, an assembler, BASIC, and a CRT display can now be purchased for about twice the cost of a microcomputer board. Throughout the remainder of this book, this is the tool we will be using.

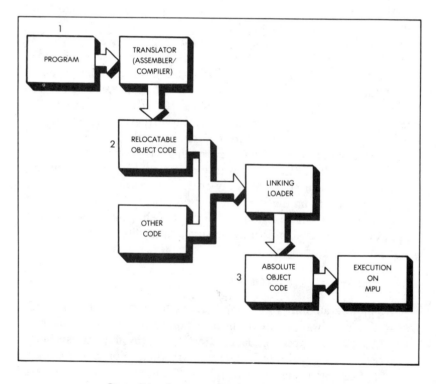

Figure 5-6: A program development sequence

EXERCISES FOR SELF-TESTING

(Answers on Next Page)

Exercise 5.1: In a flowchart, if several arrows lead into a box, is the box necessarily diamond-shaped?

Exercise 5.2: Can there be more than one arrow leaving a rectangle?

Exercise 5.3: What is the hexadecimal representation of "10101010"?

ANSWERS FOR SELF-TESTING EXERCISES

Exercise 5.1: No.

Exercise 5.2: No.

Exercise 5.3: "AA."

6

FROM BASIC TO COBOL

INTRODUCTION

High-level languages have been invented to facilitate writing computer programs. These languages are composed of English-like statements that specify sequences of computer operations. To avoid ambiguity, all high-level languages follow a strict syntax. Each language has been designed for programming in one or more of the different fields of applications, such as science, business or education. As a result, there is no "best" programming language, only a number of different languages, some of which are best-suited for a category of users, a class of problems, or a set of computers.

In the case of microcomputers, two specific restrictions have limited the number of programming languages available. First, the limited amount of memory and the frequent absence of a disk require languages that can be implemented efficiently in a small amount of memory. Second, a high-level language necessitates the development of a compiler or interpreter that translates high-level instructions into sequences of binary operations that the computer can execute. Writing a compiler or an interpreter for a new computer is very costly. There must be a large demand in order to cover such development costs.

When microcomputers first appeared, only two high-level languages were made available: BASIC and PL/M. BASIC was selected, because it is easy to learn and use, and can be implemented in a small amount of memory (4K to 16K, depending upon its "completeness.") It quickly became the dominant language for personal computers. PL/M (trademark) was developed by Intel to facilitate writing programs in the field of industrial control, and has been used widely. However, as the cost of disks and memory decreased, and as the number of users grew, other languages were introduced.

PASCAL is a recently developed language that provides more powerful capabilities than BASIC, and is now widely used.

COBOL is the traditional language in which the overwhelming

majority of business programs have been written, on larger computers.

FORTRAN is the grandfather of many languages, and has been used in the past for the majority of scientific applications.

APL is a powerful language well-suited for mathematical and business applications but requiring a scientific background.

As microcomputers grow in volume and in technical capabilities, still more languages will be introduced.

The purpose of this chapter is to review the basic characteristics of the most important languages. We will show that each language has advantages and disadvantages which must be evaluated by the user. The descriptions presented here should facilitate such a choice, as well as give the reader a feeling for the language.

BASIC

BASIC is a "high-level" programming language. It is an acronym for "Beginner's All-purpose Symbolic Instruction Code," and was developed at Dartmouth College. Essentially, a reduced version of the venerable FORTRAN language, the BASIC language can be easily learned by non-specialists in a matter of hours. Further, BASIC is normally executed by an "interpreter": each instruction can be executed as soon as it is typed (the language is said to be "interactive"). The computer will immediately detect and indicate a syntax error, allowing immediate correction.

Let us look at some practical examples, and observe the programming rules.

```
10    PRINT "THE SUM OF 2 + 3 IS" 2 + 3
20    END
```

Each line is an instruction. The execution of this simple program is obtained by typing "RUN", and results in:

THE SUM OF 2 + 3 IS 5

Each program is terminated by an "END" statement. Each instruction is preceded by a "label": the numbers 10 or 20 in the example above. The label is required to sort out instructions in order. For example, if we want to add a new instruction, we can type:

```
9    PRINT "THIS IS AN ADDITION"
```

The new instruction is then automatically inserted into the program before the instruction labeled "10". The new program is:

```
 9    PRINT "THIS IS AN ADDITION"
10    PRINT "THE SUM OF 2 + 3 IS" 2 + 3
20    END
```

The use of labels makes it possible to add new instructions at any time. For flexibility, it is traditional to label successive instructions initially as 10, 20, 30, etc., so that additional multiple instructions can be easily added.

Instruction 10 performed an *arithmetic operation* in our example. BASIC can perform five types of operations:

$$+, -, *, /, **, \text{ or } \uparrow$$

Note: " + " and " − " are the usual plus and minus; "*" and "/" represent multiply and divide; " ↑ " or "**" represents a power, depending upon the way that the system's printer prints special characters. In addition, parentheses may be used to specify groupings and the order in which operations must be performed.

Our sample program also shows two types of instructions:
— Executable instructions (such as PRINT)
— System commands (such as END or RUN)
Let us now expand this program:

```
10    LET A = 2
20    LET B = 3
30    LET S = A + B
40    PRINT "THE SUM OF A + B IS" S
50    END
```

The result is the same as before. "A", "B", and "S" are called *variables*. The "LET" instruction assigns the value 2 to A, and 3 to B, then computes A + B and assigns the value of the sum to S.

Variables in BASIC must include only one letter, and may be followed by an optional digit. This is formalized by: [variable] = [letter] ([digit]) where ( ) denotes the optional contents. (This is called "BNF Notation," or "Backus-Naur form," and is a formal way of describing the syntax of a language.)

Note: the word "LET" is a remnant of the past. Older, "pure" BASICs use it. It is totally unnecessary and needlessly cumbersome. The most recent BASICs have dispensed with the explicit "LET". The other rules remain the same.

How are numbers represented? Pure BASIC allows both integers and decimal numbers. Unfortunately, many microcomputer BASICs provide only integer numbers! This is a significant drawback.

It is also important to check the number of digits that are provided. 6 digits are an absolute minimum, and the 6 digits will not allow the representation of amounts greater than $9999.99.

Reading Values

BASIC provides two statements to read values: "READ" and "INPUT".

"READ" is used together with a "DATA" statement, and will assign a value listed as "DATA" to a variable.

In the example:

```
10    DATA 2
20    READ A
```

the result is A = 2.

Multiple variables may also be listed:

```
10    DATA 2, 3, 4, 5, 6
20    READ A, B, C, D, E
```

"INPUT" will read a number from the keyboard. The program will stop, and a "?" will appear on the display. The user must type a number, and terminate with a "carriage return" (special character: CR). The value is then automatically read by the program, and it proceeds. For example:

```
The computer reads the instruction:
     10    INPUT A(CR)
The computer responds:
     ?
The user types:
     24(CR)
The program proceeds, with A now equal to 24.
```

Comments

We would now like to clarify our program by writing comments in it.

This is possible with the REM instruction:

```
10   REM THIS PROGRAM WILL DOUBLE A NUMBER
20   INPUT A
30   PRINT "DOUBLE IS" 2*A
40   GO TO 20
```

The fourth instruction is new. It is a "GO TO" instruction, which specifies that, instead of executing the next sequential instruction, the program will "go back to instruction 20" and "INPUT A" again.

Note that the program will not stop by itself. You will have to interrupt it. This is called an infinite loop. Ordinarily, there should not be any infinite loops in a program.

Let us now look at another program:

```
10   REM SALES TAX COMPUTATION
20   INPUT P
30   REM USER NOW TYPES THE PURCHASE PRICE
40   T = P*6.5/100
50   PRINT "TAX AT 6.5% IS" T
60   PRINT "PLEASE PAY" (P + T)
70   PRINT
80   GO TO 20
```

(Instruction 70 is used to insert a blank line.)

Scientific Notation

In order not to waste space (and time) on paper, BASIC will print decimal numbers in a normalized fashion, called scientific notation:

$$E + 05 \text{ represents } 10^5$$

"E", in this example, is called the exponent.

Testing Conditions

The true power of a program does not so much lie in its arithmetic capability as it does in its capability to base decisions upon the results of tests. Special instructions are provided to that effect:

```
10   IF A = 1 THEN 50
```

The above instruction means: if A is equal to 1, then execute instruction 50 ("GO TO 50").

The IF . . . THEN . . . instruction is quite powerful. Six relational operators may be used with this instruction:

$=$ (equal to)
$<$ (less than)
$>$ (greater than)
$>=$ (greater than or equal to)
$<=$ (less than or equal to)
$<>$ (not equal to)

In addition, a complete arithmetic expression may follow the "IF", and a command may follow the "THEN".

Automating Loops

It is frequently necessary to repeat an operation until a condition is met. This can be done by using the "IF" . . . "THEN" instruction. However, if a variable is being regularly incremented, a more efficient facility exists: this is the "DO-LOOP", implemented with the "FOR" . . . "NEXT" instruction.

For example:

```
10   REM PRINT NUMBERS FROM 1 TO 50
20   FOR A = 1 TO 50
30   PRINT A
40   NEXT A
50   END
```

This program assigns the value "1" to A, then prints it. Instruction 40 ("NEXT A") automatically:

— Increments A by 1: A becomes equal to 2.
— Forces a "branch to the FOR", i.e., to instruction 20. The program loops until A reaches 50. When A = 50, instruction 40 will fail, as A will have exceeded its specified range ("50"), and the next sequential instruction will be executed: "END". The program then terminates.

Loops like those just described may be nested within one another as long as they do not overlap:

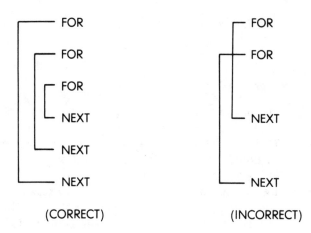

FOR	FOR
FOR	FOR
FOR	
NEXT	NEXT
NEXT	
NEXT	NEXT
(CORRECT)	(INCORRECT)

Built-In Functions

We would like to provide more arithmetic facilities, but all available characters are already utilized. This problem is solved by providing 3-character functions:

> INT( ), SQR( ), ABS( ), SGN( )
> INT is the integer value: INT $(-2.5) = -2$
> SQR is the square root
> ABS is the absolute value: ABS $(-2.5) = 2.5$
> SGN is the sign: $+1$ for a positive number
> -1 for a negative number
>   0 for 0

Subroutines

A subroutine is a program segment written as a separate unit, which may be "used" repeatedly in the main program, by calling it. An example:

```
(MAIN PROGRAM)

50     GOSUB 150
60     • • •
•
•
•
```

```
150   (SUBROUTINE)
  •
  •
  •
200   RETURN
```

Step 50 will cause execution to "jump" to statement 150. The subroutine will then be executed until "RETURN" is encountered. When RETURN is found, execution will "return to the main program." The next instruction to be executed will be instruction 60, i.e., the instruction following the subroutine call.

Conceptually, the subroutine is inserted during execution at the place of the call. This saves having to explicitly write this subroutine every time that it is needed in the main program. A mere "GOSUB" obtains the same result.

User-Defined Functions

BASIC allows a user to define his or her own functions, using a DEF FN instruction:

DEF FN(X) = [expression]

Lists and Arrays

Usually BASIC provides only two structures: one-dimensional lists, and two-dimensional arrays.

The following program will read 10 numbers typed at the keyboard, and then print them in sequence:

```
10   FOR I = 1 TO 10
20   INPUT L[I]
30   NEXT I
40   PRINT L[1]; L[2]; . . . ; L[10]
```

The "FOR. . .TO" instruction specifies a LOOP: "I" starts with the value 1, and will be incremented by step 30. After step 30, the next instruction is step 10 until I reaches 10. When it does, the next instruction after 30 will be 40 (end of loop).

Example

The following program reads 10 numbers from the keyboard, and then computes the sum:

```
20    S = 0
30    FOR I = 1 TO 10
40    INPUT A [I]
50    S = S + A[1]
60    NEXT I
70    PRINT "THE SUM IS"; S
```

The reader should verify this program by sequencing it by hand. S is the sum. It starts with a value of zero (step 20), then is incremented by the value of each successive element (A[I]) read from the keyboard (step 50) during the loop (steps 30, 40, 50, 60), and then is finally printed (step 70).

Modified Example

The following program will first type out the 10 numbers, then the total T:

```
10     REM COMPUTE TOTAL OF SALES TODAY FOR 10 ITEMS
20     FOR I = 1 TO 10
40     INPUT A[I]
50     NEXT I
60     PRINT "INDIVIDUAL SALES TODAY ARE:"
70     FOR J = 1 TO 10
80     PRINT A[J];
90     NEXT J
100    REM COMPUTE TOTAL NOW
110    T = 0
120    FOR K = 1 TO 10
130    T = T + S[K]
140    NEXT K
150    PRINT "TOTAL IS"; T
END
```

A Business Tabulation

Let us list the number of items sold for all ten items of the inventory. The DATA statement lists the items sold during the day.

N[I] represents the number of items sold for each item I.

```
10     REM SET ALL N'S TO ZERO
20     FOR I = 1 TO 10
```

```
30    LET N[I] = 0
40    NEXT I
50    READ Q
60    REM TEST FOR LIST OF ITEMS SOLD EXHAUSTED
70    IF Q = 0 THEN 100
80    LET N[Q] = N[Q] + 1
90    GO TO 50
100   PRINT "TOTAL SALES PER ITEM ARE"
110   FOR I = 1 TO 10
120   PRINT I, N[I]
130   NEXT I
200   DATA 2, 1, 1, 1, 8, 7, 3, 4, 5, 9, 1, 2, 1, 0
999   END
RUN
```

TOTAL SALES PER ITEM ARE:

1	5
2	2
3	1
4	1
5	1
6	0
7	1
8	1
9	1
10	0

Special Facilities

BASIC also provides instructions for operating on matrices, strings, and files, as well as an optional format specification ("TAB") of the output.

Most BASICs also allow multiple statements on a single line, separated by "&", ";", or "/", in addition to multiple assignments such as: X, Y, Z = 0.

Finally, REM is often replaced by an "*" or by quoted comments.

How Complete Is Your BASIC?

Although BASIC is, in theory, standard, no two BASICs are entirely alike. The major differences to be found (i.e., the facilities most often missing in some BASICs) are:

— Availability of decimal numbers. While this may seem surprising, most "mini-BASICs" only provide integer arithmetic.
— Number of digits used to represent numbers. Six is an absolute minimum. Nine may be adequate. More would be desirable.
— Availability of a file system, so that data and programs can be automatically retrieved from a disk or other support.
— Both sequential and random access files (sequential files are used on tapes, random files on disks).
— Formatting instructions (on output).
— Full string manipulation capabilities.
— A built-in editor that is powerful enough to edit the program conveniently, i.e., insert, append, modify, search for pattern, etc.

Facilities that can be added to improve on BASIC are:
— A hardware floating-point board (FPB). This special board speeds up arithmetic operations by a factor of 10 or more.
— CALL to machine-language programs. In this way, the most-often-used segments of a program can be coded in assembler, converted to object-code ("machine language"), and used by the BASIC program, resulting in a high execution speed.

In summary, the deficiencies most often found on various BASIC implementations are incomplete input-output capabilities, string handling, and high-precision decimal arithmetic.

Business BASIC

"Business BASIC" refers to a complete BASIC, equipped with additional data processing capabilities (primarily text-processing). Typical additional facilities may include:
1. Binary integers (often indicated by the % symbol).
2. Extended precision arithmetic (12- to 18-digit accuracy). It is important to remember that a computer truncates numbers internally, therefore, digits may be lost in any arithmetic operation. The computation of error propagation is beyond the scope of this book. However, the computation $3 \times \frac{1}{3}$ may not give "1" as a result, but 0.999999999, for example. Most business computations perform only simple arithmetic. In such cases, the truncation error is minimal, and often close to, or actually zero. For an acceptable precision in the result, it is important to carry internally as many digits as possible. Ten digits is probably an absolute minimum for business applications. Eighteen is highly desirable.

Caution: Before using a "BASIC" for business purposes, we strongly suggest that you perform some computations that take into account the worst possible case, and observe the precision of the results.

3. More formats. In business applications, it is essential to generate suitably formatted reports or data for form printing. The availability of convenient commands is therefore important. Standard BASIC, like FORTRAN, is noted for awkwardness and difficulty in handling and formatting text.

4. Strings of blanks. The ability to conveniently specify strings of blanks is an important facility for positioning text across a page.

5. Sub-string search. When searching a list for the occurrence of a name or a code, the program is searching a string of a "sub-string." The commands that automate this procedure greatly facilitate, or even make feasible such applications. Any update in a list, for example, will search for sub-strings in order to alphabetize or check them for duplication.

6. Assignment of strings. When manipulating strings, there must be a capability that handles them like any data (i.e., names them, assigns them to other variables, and modifies their contents.) Modification of contents may involve truncation, concatenation (adding new text), inserting, or substitution.

How Fast Is Your BASIC?

The efficiency of the *interpreter* program that implements BASIC is a key factor. Of course, the speed of the microprocessor itself plays a significant role, however, a sloppily designed interpreter can easily operate ten times slower than a professional one.

Many manufacturers rush to market with a sloppily designed "mini-BASIC" that works correctly but slowly, and is incomplete. Other manufacturers offer a new, complete, or almost complete version of BASIC (with improvements). It is therefore difficult to assess the speed of a BASIC interpreter.

This can, however, be done by using "benchmark programs." A *benchmark program* is a "typical" program written by the user for his/her intended application. The user runs this program on several different computers in order to gain numbers on which to base a comparison. This process can be painstaking, as instructions may have to be "slightly" modified in order for the same program to run with various BASIC interpreters.

Compiled BASIC

The relative inefficiency (from a speed standpoint) of a BASIC interpreter is intrinsic to all interpreters. Recall that an *interpreter* translates every instruction into machine executable format, and executes it immediately. Once a statement is executed, nothing remains, except the result of the operation.

Most programs use *loops* that are executed several times. In a loop, every statement is translated, and then executed "n" times, if the loop is executed "n" times. This is thoroughly inefficient in terms of speed.

A *compiler,* on the other hand, translates the entire user program once into machine executable format (object-code), which can then be executed at any time. The object-code can result in repeated executions of a loop, without the need to repeatedly translate statements; therefore, execution is much faster.

However, once the translation is performed, it becomes very difficult to add, modify or delete statements, and the entire program must be translated again (a lengthy process). For this reason, compilers are normally not used in an *interactive* environment. In fact, BASIC was developed specifically as an *interpretive* version of the FORTRAN language (FORTRAN is compiled). There are now systems that provide a compiled BASIC in addition to the regular interpreter. The speed benefits can be significant (several times faster, depending on the program and the efficiency of the compiler).

This facility is valuable for finished programs, which are not going to be modified for a while. The interpreter is still highly desirable for all development.

The Limitations of BASIC

While BASIC is by far one of the easiest languages to use, it is not complete:
— Its arithmetic capabilities are restricted by the limited built-in functions, the limited precision, and the slowness of execution. It can also only handle 2-dimensional arrays.
— Its string-handling capabilities are minimal, making it difficult to manipulate lists of information, such as chains of characters, or more complete structures.
— The syntax of the language does not allow complex block structures to be built: the result is a significant limitation on the complexity of the programs which can be written.

SUMMARY OF BASIC STATEMENTS

DATA	Used with READ to store values of variables, separated by commas.
GOSUB N	Subroutine call. Subroutine is executed up to RETURN.
END	Last statement in a program. May be optional.
FOR I = A TO B STEP C	Loop instruction. Step is optional.
DEF FNX(Y)	Function definition. "X" is name of function. "Y" is argument.
DIM A(X)	Dimension for array "A" (may be 2-dimensional).
GO TO n	Specifies instruction "n" as the next one to be executed.
IF x THEN y	The logical test "x" is performed. If successful, instruction "y" is executed. Otherwise, the next sequential instruction is executed.
INPUT	Causes data to be read from the keyboard up to a "CR" (carriage return).
LET	Assignment statement (often optional). Multiple assignments may usually be strung on a line.
MAT	Matrix instructions.
PRINT	Prints values or text, separated by commas or semi-colons.
NEXT I	End of a loop. Increments I and returns to the previous FOR instruction.
READ	Used with DATA to assign value to variables.
REM	Remark inserted in a program (non-executable).

RESTORE   Restores DATA statements to their first item.

RETURN   Last instruction executed in a subroutine. Causes a
               "return" to the next instruction following the GOSUB.

STOP   Halts execution of the program. Replaces END in
               some systems.

OTHER BASIC FACILITIES

MAT: A variety of matrix instructions.

FUNCTIONS: Predefined functions such as ABS(X), RND(X),
               SGN(X), SQR(X), SIN(X), COS(X), TAN(X),
               LOG(X), EXP(X), TAB(X).

FILES facilities: For naming files, reading, writing, inserting, ap-
               pending, resetting file pointers. Files may be ASCII,
               binary, sequential, formatted, or random-access.

ALTERNATIVES TO BASIC

Historically, the only "alternative" to BASIC has been PL/M.
PL/M is trademarked by Intel Corporation and stands for "Programming Language for Microprocessors." It is a compiled language
derived from the PL/I language of IBM, or more precisely, from the
XPL dialect.

As a high-level language, PL/M offers the classic advantages over
machine-level language: programs are easier and faster to write. Of
course, it also has the inherent disadvantage of any high-level language:
execution is significantly slower, and programs are longer than in
machine-level language.

PL/M was the first high-level language to be made available for
microprocessors. Many manufacturers provide a version of PL/M,
under various names such as MPL, XPLM, or SMPL. PL/M is used
to advantage in a number of industrial applications. However, PL/M
is relatively complex, difficult to use, has only integer arithmetic, and
is a compiler. It is generally not used for personal or business applications.

The next question is: "Is there a better alternative to BASIC?"
Several important alternatives exist: APL, PASCAL, FORTRAN and
COBOL.

APL

APL, a language originally invented by Iverson, has gained slow, but ever-increasing recognition. APL is considered by some to be one of the languages best-suited for scientific and business applications.

APL has several advantages:

1. APL is self-teaching. The rules of APL's syntax are so simple and clear that anyone can start writing simple programs in an hour or two, just by sitting at a terminal and "talking to the machine." APL is highly interactive, and syntax errors are immediately detected as they are typed.

2. APL is very powerful. APL uses special operators and can perform highly complex operations on virtually any structure. It can even transpose a matrix with a special operator (an n-dimensional matrix). Highly complex programs can be expressed in just a few instructions. In particular, APL has been found to be an almost ideal language for business applications, and is often used at business schools.

3. APL is a true "lambda language." Without detailing lambda calculus principles, we will say that APL allows the user to write structured programs of unrestricted complexity, communicating through predefined variables or structures.

Of course, APL also has disadvantages:

1. It uses a special character set. APL operators use a variety of symbols (such as □, Δ, and ι), not available on many displays or printers.

2. APL programs are sometimes condensed to the point where they are undecipherable. This is the result of the very power of the language. This problem can be solved by better programming habits and good documentation.

3. It is very difficult to develop an efficient APL interpreter. This is reflected in the scarcity of APL interpreters and software.

Simple Examples

Here are some simple examples of APL instructions.

— This one adds two "vectors":

    1 2 3 4 5 + 2 3 4 5 6

and results in: 3 5 7 9 1 1

— This simple arithmetic:

$$2 \times 3$$

prints: 6

— and,

$$1 + 2 + 3 + 4$$

prints: 10

— A print command:

'HELLO'

prints: HELLO

— Powerful operators:

!6

represents factorial 6, i.e., $1 \times 2 \times 3 \times 4 \times 5 \times 6$;

$\lfloor 2.3$

is the floor of 2.3, i.e., 2; and

$\iota\, 5$ (iota five)

generates the vector 1 2 3 4 5

A Complex Example

The factorial of "n" is defined by:

$$n! = 1 \times 2 \times 3 \times \ldots \times n$$

which is simply the product of the "n" first numbers. The following APL program computes the factorial of "n":

∇ Z ←FAC N
[1] ⭢ 4* ι N = 0
[2] Z ← N* FAC N − 1
[3] ⭢ 0
[4] Z ← 1
∇

The first line of this program is a "function" definition. The function is started and terminated by the special symbol ∇ (delta). The name of the function is FAC. Its parameter is the variable N, and its result is the variable Z.

[1] Specifies: GO TO 4 if N = 0 (the combination * ι may be read as "if").

[2] Specifies: take the value of N multiplied by FAC of (N − 1). FAC(N − 1) is a function call within the function FAC. This is a *recursive* call, where a function calls itself. The result is the function FAC being reentered for execution with a parameter (N − 1).

[3] Means "GO TO step 0", i.e., go out (return from the function). This terminates function execution. At this point, Z should contain the value of the factorial.

[4] Assigns the value 1 to Z.

∇ is the end of the function. It also terminates function execution.

Exercise 6-1: FAC 3 should result in Z = 6. Try it by hand, and follow the execution step-by-step.

APL Summary

APL is a powerful language that allows complex programs to be written in fewer instructions. However, APL requires a good background in mathematics and, therefore, tends to be used by specific professions only.

APL also requires a large memory space and a powerful processor. It is therefore more likely to be used on systems equipped with a hard disk and a fast microprocessor.

FORTRAN

FORTRAN, the oldest scientific programming language, stands for "FORmula TRANslator." Although FORTRAN is cumbersome, difficult to implement, and inefficient, it is still used. A huge library exists of scientific programs written in FORTRAN.

FORTRAN requires a fast processor and a large memory space. For this reason, FORTRAN has been replaced by BASIC in the world of 8-bit microprocessors. FORTRAN compilers are, however, available, so that existing FORTRAN programs can be run on small computers. FORTRAN is a language that is likely to be used more often in the future, for scientific applications, on systems equipped with a hard disk and a 16-bit microprocessor.

PASCAL

The programming language FORTRAN originally gained widespread acceptance in scientific applications. BASIC, which evolved from the FORTRAN language, was designed to be simple to learn and easy to use. BASIC is not, however, efficient from the computer's standpoint, as it consumes a great deal of execution time, and is limited in the complexity of the applications that can be handled efficiently.

PASCAL evolved from the ALGOL language, which was utilized primarily in education and research. Used extensively in teaching computer programming, PASCAL differs from BASIC in that it is a more powerful and complex language, and can actually be executed more quickly. In PASCAL, the structure and type of all identifiers must be specified, whereas a BASIC program simply specifies a sequence of actions to be performed.

PASCAL was invented in 1970-71 by Niklaus Wirth of the ETH Technical Institute in Zurich, Switzerland. Examples of PASCAL programs will now be shown in order to demonstrate its particular characteristics.

A Pascal Program

Here is an example of a simple PASCAL program:

```
PROGRAM AVERAGE (INPUT, OUTPUT);
VAR
        A, B, AVERAGE: REAL;
BEGIN
        READ (A, B);
        AVERAGE = (A + B)/2;
        WRITELN ('THE AVERAGE OF', A, 'AND', B, 'IS', AVERAGE)
END.
```

The name of the program ("AVERAGE") is explicitly declared in the program header on the first line. The program header also specifies that "INPUT" and "OUTPUT" will be used in program implementation.

The variables "A", "B", and "AVERAGE" are declared of type "REAL" in the second line of the program. "A" and "B" might also have been of type "INTEGER"; however, since there is no guarantee that the result will be an integer, the average (or result) is always of type "REAL".

This formal type declaration is typical of PASCAL. The compiler, which translates a sequence of instructions into a set of binary codes that the computer can execute, is able to allocate storage more efficiently and handle each type specifically when it receives a type declaration. Type declaration is also advantageous to the programmer, since every time values are assigned to these variables, the compiler will automatically check to see that their type is correct (in this case, of type "REAL").

PASCAL is structured in blocks. The above program includes one block, delimited by the reserved word, "BEGIN" and "END". This block includes three statements. The first will read the values of "A" and "B" typed at the keyboard. The second will compute the value of the "AVERAGE", while the third will print the value of this average ("WRITELN").

Following is another example of a PASCAL program that computes the nth power of x, where x is a "REAL" (decimal) number, and n is an integer:

```
!
PROGRAM XPOWERN(INPUT,OUTPUT);
VAR
    X           :  REAL;       (* BASE PART OF NO. TO BE
                                  RAISED *)
    N           :  INTEGER;    (* EXPONENT NO. IS TO BE RAISED
                                  TO*)
    ANSWER      :  REAL;       (* X ** N *)
    CALCULATING :  BOOLEAN;    (* TRUE WHILE USER WANTS TO
                                  CONTINUE WITH CALCULA-
                                  TIONS *)

(* THE FOLLOWING FUNCTION FINDS THE VALUE OF X TO THE NTH
POWER *)
```

```
FUNCTION POWER(X : REAL; N : INTEGER):REAL;
BEGIN
    IF N = 1 THEN                                    (*     1     *)
        POWER : = X                                  (* I.E. X = X *)
    ELSE
        POWER : = X * POWER(X,N−1)
END;


BEGIN
    CALCULATING : = TRUE;
    WHILE CALCULATING DO BEGIN
        WRITELN('':38,'N');
        WRITELN('THIS PROGRAM DETERMINES THE VALUE OF X .');
        WRITELN('PLEASE ENTER X AND N − ENTER 0 0 TO END');
        WRITE('PROGRAM');
        READLN(X,N);
        IF (X = 0) AND (N = 0) THEN
            CALCULATING : = FALSE
        ELSE BEGIN              (* IF USER WANTS TO CONTINUE *)
            IF N = 0 THEN    (*     0     *)
                ANSWER : = 1 (*I.E. X = 1 *)
            ELSE
                ANSWER : = POWER(X,ABS(N));
            IF N < 0 THEN                        (*     −N     N*)
                ANSWER : = 1 / ANSWER;        (* I.E. X = 1/X *)
            WRITELN('':14,'N');
            WRITELN('THE VALUE OF X = ',ANSWER)
        END; (* IF *)
    END; (* WHILE *)
END.
```

Note the type declarations at the beginning of the program, followed by the definition of a function ("POWER"), and the main program. Also, note the indentations used to clarify the program every time that a modifier is used, such as: "WHILE", "IF", and "ELSE".

These two examples are relatively similar to the way that they could have been written in BASIC (except for the type declarations). PASCAL, however, is block-oriented, and provides a number of complex types, including structure specifications. These facilities are more involved, and beyond the scope of this introductory chapter.

PASCAL is much more powerful than BASIC, and, therefore, more difficult to learn. For the casual programmer, BASIC should be sufficient in most instances. For the person interested in studying programming languages or designing complex programs, PASCAL is an excellent educational tool.

COBOL

COBOL (Common Business Oriented Language) is the language that has been used by the overwhelming majority of business programs on large computers. The wealth of programs written in COBOL appear to make it a prime candidate as a microcomputer language.

A COBOL program includes up to four parts:

— The *Identification Division* identifies the program.
— The *Environment Division* specifies the computer hardware and the peripherals on which files are stored.
— The *Data Division* specifies the data used as files, constants or temporary storage.
— The *Procedure Division* specifies the program proper, i.e., the sequence of instructions.

Both the Data Division and the Procedure Division require careful design. For example, the Data Division includes up to four sections:

— The file section (input and output)
— The working storage section (temporary data)
— The linkage section (a common area shared by two or more programs)
— The report section (output formatting)

The language has been designed for convenient text and data manipulation and offers very limited arithmetic capabilities.

A COBOL compiler is much larger and more complex than a BASIC interpreter. Most COBOL programs have been designed for larger computers with disks. The recent availability of low-cost fixed-head Winchester-type disks, however, has solved the space problem. COBOL is now available on many microcomputers, and its role will increase in the future.

WHAT ABOUT "NATURAL LANGUAGE"?

Of course, the most desirable language for communicating with a computer is an ordinary, spoken language (English, for example). It would be most practical for the human user to "program" directly in English. In fact, during the heyday of NASA and the space race, the

U.S. govenment funded extensive research programs to determine the feasibility of using English, or a suitable subset, as a programming language. The results were totally unequivocal: ordinary English cannot be used.

The problem is ambiguity. The spoken language is not precise enough to be unequivocal, and relies on context to specify the meaning of a sentence. The context may be sensory (gesture, odor, etc.) or syntactic (i.e., depending on what was said before, or will be said next). The processing that is needed to resolve these ambiguities would simply use up all of a computer's resources, and with no absolute assurance of success. Such an approach is, therefore, totally inefficient.

For this reason, it was felt that a well-defined subset of the English language with a "clean syntax" must be used: a programming language. A variety of programming languages have been developed that appeal to specific classes of users, depending upon their training. BASIC has been identified as an easy one to use. This explains the success of BASIC in the microcomputer world.

Let us summarize: there is no hope that a computer will be able to understand ordinary English in the forseeable future. Therefore, any claim to "Direct English Programming" is deliberately misleading. Such systems simply use some programming language, with the usual syntactic limitations.

This does not, however, rule out the possibility of "talking to the computer" by using a well-defined subset of the English language and fixed rules. In this case, one is simply defining still another high-level programming language.

SUMMARY

BASIC is currently the most widely used language on small computers. It is used for most commercial programs.

FORTRAN is a relic of the past, cumbersome and inefficient, but useful for scientific applications because of the wealth of programs available.

PASCAL has gained wide recognition in the educational field and is increasingly used for complex programs.

APL has had limited success, due to the difficulties of its implementation and the special character set.

COBOL is the most widely-used language on larger computers but is not yet used significantly on microcomputers. New business programs for small computers are usually written in BASIC.

PL/M and similar high-level languages are used in the industrial field.

Computer Education

7

BUSINESS COMPUTING

INTRODUCTION

Complete business computing capabilities can now be obtained through a low-cost microcomputer system. Since computers were first introduced, the main limitations of such systems have not been at the hardware level but at the software level. The hardware necessary to efficiently process a number of business applications is available and can be purchased for $5,000 to $20,000. Good software, however, is just beginning to appear on the market.

Many compromises must be made to obtain the capabilities that a user may wish to acquire. These compromises will be discussed in this chapter. In order to define the processing capabilities that are required to achieve specific business goals, the classic applications of computers in business will be reviewed first.

To be able to make a reasonable selection of a computer system, the purchaser must understand the trade-offs between the various choices available today, as there is no "best choice." The selection process can be compared to that of choosing a new car, or a complex machine to be used for a specific application. There is no all-around system that will fit all business applications and still be inexpensive.

Understanding the hardware required and the hardware available is a relatively simple matter. Understanding the software capabilities required and the software available is more complex. It is usually during the purchase of a business system that mistakes are made. Software mistakes are generally more costly than those made during hardware selection.

Not only does the investment in software often become the most expensive investment, but, more importantly, inadequate software will limit the potential growth of the capabilities of the system, and possibly the business itself. A transition to a different system might be costly and disruptive. For these reasons, the reader is strongly encouraged to study and understand the software as well as the hardware concepts presented in this chapter.

APPLICATIONS OF COMPUTERS IN BUSINESS

Every business needs to maintain a number of files. Some files that are frequently used include: accounts receivable, accounts payable, inventory, and general ledger. Additional files that are usually desirable include: personnel, customer list, mailing list, back-order lists, sales lists, vendor list, cash situation, company property, and more. These lists are managed either by hand (usually by a bookkeeper), or with the help of electro-mechanical devices, a computer, or a combination of these devices.

In addition to maintaining files, every business also applies specific *processing* techniques. For example, a *payroll program* will process the *personnel file* and generate payroll reports, as well as print checks. A *tax program* will process the *sales reports* and the *personnel files* to produce the required *tax reports*. A *transaction procedure* program will manage updates of specific files, and changes or entry of new data. A typical example is a new sale: the transaction program will utilize the inventory file, supplier file, customer file, as well as other files. It will update them, and print reports.

Similarly, an *incoming shipment procedure* will handle shipments coming in, enter them into the inventory file, check for back orders, and add entries to the accounts payable list.

Any payment received will update the *accounts receivable* and *cash situation* files. Figure 7-1 illustrates these lists, and typical processing programs. Arrows indicate the effect of a specific action on the various files in the system.

Besides the main programs, which are shown in the illustration as circles, a number of additional programs are required to produce useful reports. These additional facilities will be described in more detail in the next few pages.

Note that the principle is quite simple:

— Files must be created and maintained
— Programs should be available to provide the interface between the user and the files, and supply the required processing functions.

Unfortunately, in a real business system, accessing a file is only part of the processing required. In fact, in most businesses, the direct maintenance of a single file is reasonably simple. The bulk of the pro-

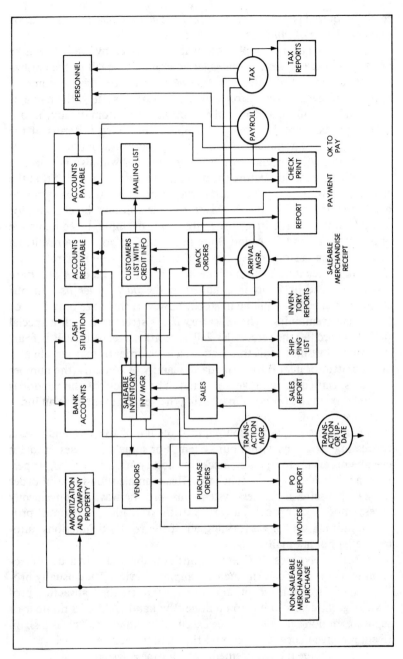

Figure 7-1: Business files and programs

cessing required is due to the simultaneous *cross-referencing* and *automatic updating* of *multiple files.*

Let us look at an example. An order is received by mail. It will be processed by the *transaction manager* program on the left of the illustration. The sale will be entered in the *sales file* for the day. A complex sequence of events now unfolds. As a result of this entry, the name of the customer will be added to the *customer list* automatically. In addition, the customer's name will probably be coded in terms of the purchase he/she has made, the amount of the purchase, or the customer's job position. His/her name or customer number will also be checked for credit information before the order is processed. Provided that the sale is not "vetoed" by the *credit manager* program, the next step is to honor the order. The *saleable inventory* file will now be checked for the availability of the items ordered. In this example, three items are ordered: A, B, and C. A and B are in stock. C is not. As a result, an *invoice* to the customer (see box at the far left of the illustration), a *shipping list* (center, bottom of the illustration), and a *back order* are generated. The back order is added to the *back order list.* In our example, item B is available in stock, however, there are only four of these items remaining. The *inventory list* is structured with a special field that specifies the reorder level. The reorder level of item B is four. As a further result of this transaction, a back order or reorder will also be generated for item B for a standard quantity of 25 items (the number 25 was specified in the inventory file). The address of the vendor is obtained from the *vendor file* by using the vendor number as an index to the list (left of illustration).

This simple sales transaction required the use of five files and several processing programs within our system. For some businesses, it might even be necessary to update, check, or modify additional files, or perform additional processing functions. This example shows that in order to be truly useful, a business system must provide ways to conveniently access, modify and process a variety of files. In addition, it must provide a mechanism for performing all of the required functions automatically, not manually.

Unfortunately, most business systems available today that use microcomputers do not perform such a complete service. They usually provide single file management, and do not complete the transaction process. A great deal still has to be done "by hand." Also, a number of separate modules may have to be executed in sequence. This is a significant inconvenience, as it requires time and trained personnel.

Let us examine the requirements of a business system.

THE REQUIREMENTS OF A BUSINESS SYSTEM

The requirements of a business system will be analyzed here in terms of the essential files that must be maintained and the necessary processing functions that must be performed.

Accounts Receivable

The accounts receivable file is essentially a file that contains a copy of all invoices generated by the system. Of course, the file does not contain the actual invoice copy, but it does contain the minimum of information necessary to allow the system to actually generate a complete invoice. Usually, the file will store the data of the transaction, the name and address of the customer, shipment point, and sales information, such as the name of the salesperson, specific details about the items sold, the manner in which the items were shipped, and the date on which the items were shipped. All of the information that appears in the usual invoice need not be stored within this *accounts receivable* file. This information can be stored in a sales file (if one exists), where it can be accessed frequently and processed efficiently.

Efficient information processing by some programs requires that all identical elements within a file be of the same length. For this reason, files that are processed by such programs often use *fixed length* entries or "blocks." For example, an accounts receivable file might be structured in that manner. Fixed fields can be allocated to essential information such as date, name, amount due, transaction or customer code, and invoice number. The presence of the invoice number allows the user of the system to access the remainder of this information in the *sales list* or in the *invoice file*. In computer jargon, the presence of a number used to access information stored elsewhere is called a *pointer*. The invoice number is used as a pointer to the actual invoice. In business jargon, this is part of the *audit trail*.

The accounts receivable *file* must be distinguished from the accounts receivable program. The accounts receivable file is simply the list of accounts. The advantages or disadvantages of its format are easily evaluated by the business user. A typical requirement is that it contain, in an easily accessible way, all of the fields that the business user requires frequently.

The accounts receivable program is responsible for manipulating this file, updating it, and generating the required report. It must also generate specialized reports such as the printing of accounts older than

30, 45, 60 or 90 days (this is called *aging*). This program can even be responsible for automatically generating *reminder notices*. However, the reminder notification program may be a separate program. In this case, the accounts receivable program would be used for generating a file of *overdue accounts*. This file would then be used in turn by the *reminder notice program* to generate personalized reminders to all customers listed in the overdue file. Whether functions are separated into individual programs or integrated within a single program has little impact on the value of this system. Its organization is largely a matter of programming convenience for the system designer. The important point is that all the facilities be readily available.

Accounts Payable

The *accounts payable file* is essentially a list of all bills or invoices received by the business, as well as any other amounts due. Usually, whenever an "OK to pay" order has been entered, the accounts payable manager program will automatically print payment checks for the goods received, or, list the amounts to be paid. Generally, the check will be printed either at a specified date, or at a programmed date such as 30 days after receipt of invoice. A good check printing program should also make sure that the cash balance in the bank account is sufficient to cover the expenditures.

Inventory

There is no optimal *inventory file,* as inventory information differs according to specific business needs. For this reason, most general-purpose inventory files carry a large number of categories, even though not all of the categories will be used by the business. The unavailability of some categories can be felt to be a drawback by some users. The availability of too many categories, on the other hand, means that a significant amount of space is wasted in the system. This translates into a smaller number of items that may be entered into the inventory. However, with the costs of memory continually decreasing, the trend now is to provide as many categories as possible for most types of businesses, even if some of them are never going to be used. Recall that the size of the inventory file is limited by the physical storage available, such as the size of a diskette.

Typical information that may be placed in an inventory file includes the following:
CODE — ITEM NUMBER — ITEM DESCRIPTION — STORAGE LOCATION — NUMBER AVAILABLE — VENDOR NUMBER —

FILLING PRICE — PURCHASE PRICE — LAST SALE DATE —
MINIMUM QUANTITY FOR REORDER.
Usually, 64 to 128 bytes at a minimum must be provided for this
type of entry. Using such a format, 1,800 to 3,600 items may be stored
in a typical diskette.

The inventory control program must provide many functions, including generalized inventory management facilities such as:
— Complete inventory maintenance, including automatic updates
of any category of information within the file
— Sales order entry
— Purchase order entry
— Sales history
— Automated back-orders
— List by quantity, class, cost, vendor, item number, date of sale
— Minimum quantity search
— Selective update
— Activity reports
— Inventory lists in function of combinations of criteria

As a rough indication, a minimal inventory management program
written in BASIC will require 10K words of memory (for all practical
purposes a "word" is a "byte" here, in the case of 8-bit microprocessors). A more general program will easily require 90K or more.
Since the central memory of a microprocessor is never larger than 64K,
an *overlay* technique is used, so that such large BASIC programs can
be run on a smaller main memory. An *overlay* consists of executing
one part of the program, then bringing an additional part of the program into the memory, and overwriting a segment (that is no longer
required) of the program installed in the main memory. The complete
BASIC program is therefore never resident in the memory in one
piece. Portions of it are brought into the central memory as needed.
Of course, this reduces the efficiency of the processing. However, if
the overlays are cleverly written, the impact on efficiency is reasonably
small.

Update

Inventory files can be updated in two ways: by hand, and automatically. Updating by hand allows the user to examine the list of
items in the inventory and modify any of the entries, such as the unit
cost, for example. The real value of the computer system, however, is
in automating the updating of identical information in many files.

Therefore, a comprehensive business system should *automatically* update the inventory file, whenever relevant information is changed somewhere else. If the unit cost of the product is changed, the inventory file, as well as any other file in which the unit cost might reside would be automatically updated.

When evaluating an inventory system, it is necessary to examine both the program and the files provided, including fields and maximum file size.

The Mailing List

The *mailing list* is often neglected in a business system, since most business systems provide a *sales list*. The sales list is a complete record of sales that usually includes the name of the customer, as well as all information relevant to the transaction. However, except for short mailings, the sales list is not the best method of listing customers for a promotional action. For long lists (such as those including several thousand names), direct processing of the sales list is completely impractical. First, it is slow, as the information in the sales list is block-structured, and only a few entries are retrieved from every block. Second, the information in the sales list is usually bulky, so that relatively few names reside on a single physical medium, such as a diskette. Processing the sales list therefore not only requires significant time, but also frequent changing of diskettes by hand.

For efficient mailing list management, the user should code every transaction at the time that it is performed, and a specific mailing list program should be available. For example, the user might code the type of business, or the type of individual involved in the transaction. The nature of the items purchased, or the range of the sale might also be coded. In this way, a compact code can be used, which can be utilized as a selection criterion within the list. An efficient mailing list is created by periodically processing the customers list, or the sales list. The list must be generally sorted, either alphabetically, by zip code, or by a special user code. In this way, whenever a new name is entered into the list, possible duplications can be checked immediately and efficiently.

Let us consider an example, in order to evaluate the storage requirements. A typical mailing list contains the first name, middle initial, last name, title, company name, division or mail stop, street or P.O. box, city, state and zip code. In addition, it will contain a five- to twenty-digit code for efficient retrieval of names (this is a minimum — even more would be desirable). All of this information results in perhaps 100 characters per entry. However, let us assume that 80 characters are sufficient for our purposes. A typical block on a diskette contains 256 characters. Using the above numbers, such a block could contain only three names. A typical diskette will provide about 1,200 such blocks, and will therefore store about 3,600 names. In practice, wider fields are often used, and an entire 256-character block may be required to store a single entry. A typical diskette will then store only 1,200 names.

A floppy disk is not convenient for storing long mailing lists. An efficient mailing list program may be capable of handling anywhere from 1,000 to 50,000 names. Clearly, a floppy-based system is very cumbersome to use, as diskettes have to be changed frequently, by hand, until the complete list is processed.

Also, when a long list is spread over several diskettes, it can only be sorted one way. For example, if the list is sorted alphabetically, names from A to L will be on one diskette, and names from M to Z on another. A single zipcode listing is impossible to obtain. Two separate listings would be generated, one per diskette. These disadvantages should be considered by the business user.

To facilitate element retrieval in a large list, a specially structured mailing list file may be required. An *index block* is created, which contains only a few bytes per entry. The index block contains the customer name or code, and a customer pointer, usually a number. In this way it can be restricted to a maximum of 20 to 30 characters. A complete diskette will usually be allocated to this mailing list index. Whenever a selection is to be performed, only the index block diskette needs to be mounted initially.

As an example, the mailing list selection is for all companies in the distribution field that have ordered more than one hundred dollars' worth of parts in the last three months. The selection program will derive all of its information from the index file and will generate a list of customer numbers meeting the specified criteria. This list can then be used by a simple mailing list printing program, which will print the addresses from the customers or sales file, as selected by the list of customer numbers. Whenever the selection has been performed, the program will start generating messages such as "please load diskette number 2-5". This diskette contains the first block of entries that the mailing list processor wants to print. If the mailing list is long, a number of diskettes will still have to be successively mounted on the system in view of the limitations inherent in each diskette. However, the complete selection, which can be a lengthy process, can be performed efficiently in a very short amount of time using only the index block diskette. A good program saves the names that it prints on a diskette, and signals the user on the CRT display that it wishes to have another specific diskette mounted next. The user will then have the time to mount the next diskette while the system is busy printing labels. By the time that the printer (which is a slow device), has finished printing the last name of the previous diskette, the new one will already have been mounted. The system performs at the maximum mechanical speed of which it is capable.

The drawback of having to feed successive diskettes to a system can be eliminated by purchasing high-capacity hard disks or dual-drive, dual-density diskette drives. New low-cost fixed-head Winchester disks are now available. Their storage capability is analogous to traditional hard disks. However, their access time is significantly slower.

Remember that many business applications are disk-limited, not processor-limited. The speed and capacity of the disk(s) may be more important than the performance of the processor.

Summary

We have examined the requirements of a business system in the case of typical business programs, such as accounts receivable, accounts payable, inventory and mailing lists.

We will now use a business system in some typical situations, in order to understand the steps involved and the facilities required. Once we have acquired this "hands-on" experience, the capabilities of existing systems and software will be evaluated in the context of these typical applications.

USING A COMPUTERIZED BUSINESS SYSTEM

First, we will go through a simulated example, in order to learn the terminology. Then we will demonstrate two actual examples: a mailing list program, and a word processing program.

In this first simulated example, we will complete a simple transaction by specifying the type of program we want, and then responding to the choices or questions appearing on the screen of the CRT terminal.

Initially, the system displays a *menu*. A menu is simply a multiple-choice question. The question asked by the system is stressed by one or more prompt characters (in this case, " . . . "), designed to indicate that the microcomputer is waiting for a response.

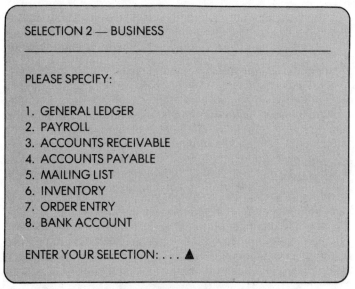

```
HELLO.
I AM YOUR COMPUTER.
WHAT DO YOU WANT TO DO?
1. GAMES
2. BUSINESS
3. APPOINTMENTS


ENTER THE NUMBER OF YOUR SELECTION:

... ▲
```

Figure 7-2:   A "menu"

We have selected the "business program." The system should load this program automatically from the disk into the memory. A directory of new options now appears (a new menu):

```
SELECTION 2 — BUSINESS


PLEASE SPECIFY:

1. GENERAL LEDGER
2. PAYROLL
3. ACCOUNTS RECEIVABLE
4. ACCOUNTS PAYABLE
5. MAILING LIST
6. INVENTORY
7. ORDER ENTRY
8. BANK ACCOUNT

ENTER YOUR SELECTION: ... ▲
```

Figure 7-3:   The business "submenu"

In response to the prompt above, we specify the "accounts receivable" file, by typing a "3". At this point, the system may request that a new diskette be inserted. Let us assume that it does not, and proceed. A new menu appears:

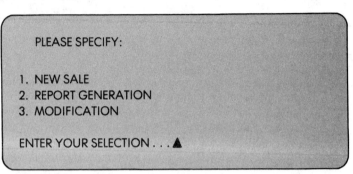

Figure 7-4:   The accounts receivable file

We specify a new sale ("1"), and the system requests all data needed to record the transaction, generate an invoice, and later update all related files such as bank, accounts receivable, inventory, and customer list. The dialogue now becomes highly interactive, with the system requesting all of the necessary data. This is illustrated in Figures 7-5, 7-6 and 7-7:

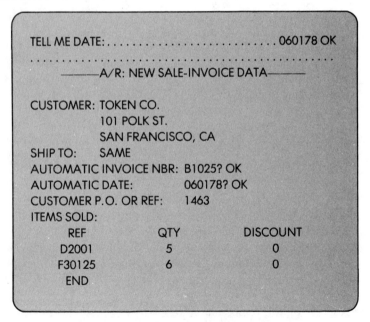

Figure 7-5:   Entering a new sale

```
ALL RIGHT PRICES ARE:
D2001              5           AT 20.00. . . . . $100.00
D30125             6           AT 30.00. . . . . $180.00
                                              _____
                   SUBTOTAL IS                    $280.00

SHIPPING CHARGES?. . . . . . . . . . . . . . . . . . . . . . .22.00
TAX EXEMPT?. . . . . . . . . . . . . . . . . . . . . . . . . . . . . . . .NO
TAX RATE?. . . . 6% . . . . . . . . . . . . . . . . . . . . . . . .16.80
TAX CODE?. . . . . . . . . . . . . . . . . . . . . . . . . . . . . . . . . .A
TOTAL DUE. . . . . . . . . . . . . . . . . . . . . . . . . . . . .$318.80
TERMS: NET 30?. . . . . . . . . . . . . . . . . . . . . . . . . .YES
```

Figure 7-6:   Sale entry (continued)

```
SALESPERSON . . . . . . . . . . . . . . . . . . . . . . . . . . . . .DR
SPECIAL COMMENTS ON INVOICE?
     NONE
SALESMAN/REP COMMISSION?                        NO
HOW SHIP? . . . . . . . . . . . . . . . . . . . . . . . . . . . . . . .UPS


     — — — — — — — — — —

TRANSACTION COMPLETED?                          YES
     — — — CREDIT CHECK REQUESTED — — —
NEXT TRANSACTION?                               NO
```

Figure 7-7:   Sale entry (end)

The transaction is completed.

The mode of interaction with the system should now be clear. The program asks all the necessary questions, and enforces a discipline.

It should also check the validity of data being entered (no gross errors). Finally, it should automatically print invoices, and later update all related files.

Let us now examine two actual examples: a mailing list program, and a word processing program.

We will demonstrate the use of these two typical business programs in a realistic environment. You will be given a feeling for the way in which a computer system is actually used, and shown how easy it is to perform various applications. First we will show how to use a mailing list program, and second we will demonstrate how a word processor can be used.

We will use a typical configuration for a business system. It is shown in Figure 7-8. This system includes the microcomputer with 64K of memory (less could be used but it would slow down the execution of the programs), two regular-sized floppy disk drives (8-inch), a CRT terminal (24 lines of 80 characters), and a daisy-wheel printer (for quality printing when using the word processor). A hard disk, highly desirable for business applications, could be added to this typical system. Let us now sit down with the operator and use the system.

THE CP/M OPERATING SYSTEM

First, the system is turned on by activating the appropriate switches on the equipment. After the system is on, our next task is to install the *operating system* inside the computer's memory. Each computer system equipped with disks is supplied with a disk-operating-system (DOS), which is stored on a disk (in this case, an 8-inch diskette). The operating system will make commands available to us for executing other programs. If there had not been a program or operating system installed in the computer's memory, the computer could not do anything. Most computer systems, however, are equipped with a small program called a *bootstrap loader* or, sometimes, a *resident monitor,* which is stored in ROM (a non-volatile type of memory which can only be read). When the computer is turned on, this short program takes over and attempts to load the operating system from the disk.

Our next task is to insert a diskette in disk drive A, as shown in Figure 7-9. This diskette is called the "system diskette," and contains the operating system in addition to other optional programs. The particular system used in this demonstration requires that we press the "return" key on the keyboard three times after inserting the diskette. Let us do it (see Figure 7-10).

A message appears on the screen of the CRT terminal, indicating that the operating system has been loaded successfully. We can now type in commands to the computer, and easily use all of its peripherals. The purpose of an operating system is to provide the user with convenient commands for executing programs and utilizing the physical

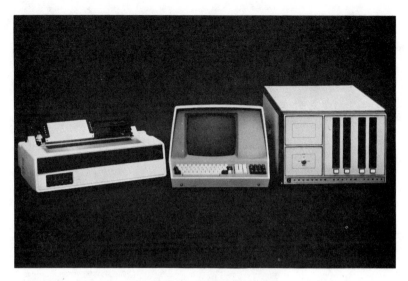

Figure 7-8:   A Cromemco system

Figure 7-9:   Inserting the system diskette

Figure 7-10: Pressing RETURN

resources of the computer system. The operating system should also provide convenient file management by allowing the user to give a name to a program or a collection of data, store it under that name on the disk, print it on the printer, or display it on the CRT.

One of the most widely used operating systems on microprocessors today is CP/M®, developed and trademarked by Digital Research. CP/M is the operating system that we will use here. The operating system on the Cromemco computer we are using is called CDOS, and will be considered identical to CP/M for the purpose of this example. Thus far, we have only been using the keyboard and CRT display as input/output devices. We do not need to use the printer yet; however, we will turn it on to keep a printed record of our procedure. In order to turn on the printer, we will press the control key, hold it down, and then press "P" *simultaneously*. This is abbreviated as "CTRL-P", a command to CP/M that means, "attach the printer." This literally connects the printer to the computer. From now on, everything that we type at the keyboard and display on the CRT screen will be typed at the printer.

Let us verify the command by using an example. We will type: DIR. This is a command to CP/M that means "directory"; it requests

CP/M to type the list of files stored on the diskette presently in drive A. We terminate our DIR command by pressing the key "return". CP/M immediately obeys our command, and displays the following list of the files stored on the diskette:

Program Name	Type	Space Used	
QSORT	COM	6K	1
NAD	INT	8K	1
NADLABEL	INT	6K	1
NADPRINT	INT	6K	1
NADENTRY	INT	9K	1
NADXTRAK	INT	5K	1
NAD	INT	3K	1
QPARM	INT	3K	1
STAT	COM	2K	1
CRUN	COM	16K	2
PIP	COM	1K	1

We can see that the diskette contains a number of programs, including the mailing list programs that we are about to use. You will also notice that the *file type* associated with each file name appears to the right of each name. This is simply intended to avoid errors, as the same name may be used for a program stored in different forms, such as the *symbolic* form and the *compiled* form.

Everything is working properly. We are now ready to use the computer and create a mailing list.

A Mailing List Program

Many commercial programs are available that will run directly on any computer equipped with CP/M. Programs have been developed to perform functions such as mailing list management, word processing, and various other business applications. We will use a mailing list program called NAD (developed and trademarked by Structured Systems of Oakland, California). This program is typical of the facilities that should be provided by a good mailing list program. NAD includes four modules: NADENTRY, NADPRINT, NADLABEL, and NADXTRAK. We will explain the purpose of these modules by using a number of examples.

In order to sort the list, two more modules will be required: QSORT and QPARM.

All of these programs are written in the BASIC language (BASIC was described in more detail in Chapter 6). Many different versions of BASIC are available today. However, the two most popular versions are probably CBASIC, a "compiled" version of BASIC used in many business applications, and MBASIC, an "interpreted" version of BASIC developed by Microsoft. All of the six programs for the mailing list management application are written in CBASIC. In order to execute them, it will be necessary to have the CBASIC compiler on the diskette. In this example, it is called CRUN. If we refer to the dictionary listing shown previously, we can verify that CRUN is indeed present on the diskette. We are now ready to execute the programs.

We type: CRUN NAD, followed by a "return". (We press the key marked "return".) By typing CRUN, the CBASIC compiler will be retrieved from the disk and executed. The compiler will then execute the program named "NAD" as specified. We will now enter five names and addresses onto this mailing list, along with the coded information. After that we will selectively retrieve the entries.

The response appears on the CRT display:

CRUN VER 2.04 +

The message "CRUN Version 2.04 +" confirms that the CRUN compiler is executing correctly.

The program also displays a "menu" on the screen:

```
    1      CREATE OR MODIFY A NAD FILE

    2      EXTRACT NAMES FROM ONE FILE TO ANOTHER

    3      PRINT A REPORT

    4      PRINT MAILING LABELS

    5      SORT BY LAST NAME

    6      SORT BY ZIP CODE

    7      CREATE NAME SRT FILE

    8      CREATE ZIP SRT FILE

    9      CHANGE SYSTEM DATE

    ESC         STOP PROGRAM

    CR          REFRESH MENU

 ENTER NUMBER OF FUNCTION DESIRED.
```

The function we desire to have performed must be specified. We type "1" as we want to create a file. The program will now "prompt us," and we answer the questions. (Note: our answers to the question are underlined.)

The program requests that a file name be specified. We type MAIL-IST. Then the program needs to know the disk drive on which the file should be stored. We indicate that disk drive B must be used. (A blank diskette has already been inserted into drive B.)

> ENTER NUMBER OF FUNCTION DESIRED 1
>
> NADPRINT
>
> ENTER FILE NAME MAILIST
>
> ENTER DRIVE (A OR B) B

The program then advises us that this file is a new file, and requests that we confirm this by typing CREATE. We comply:

FILE: MAILIST .NAD DOES NOT EXIST ON DRIVE B

TYPE 'CREATE' TO CONTINUE OR
RETURN TO ENTER NEW FILE NAME <u>CREATE</u>

This program allows us to use a variable-length *reference field*. The reference field is the sequence of characters corresponding to the codes that we wish to associate with every name and address. In this example, we will not use more than 20 characters per name. This is the length of our reference field:

ENTER LENGTH OF REFERENCE FIELD

ENTER ZERO IF NOT WANTED <u>20</u>

REFERENCE FIELD LENGTH: 20

TOTAL RECORD LENGTH: 148

128 characters are allocated by this program for the name and address. This is convenient as it corresponds to the *sector*, i.e., the unit of information on the disk. An additional 20 characters are allocated for the reference field. The program then confirms that the total record length used by the program will now be 148.

The program then asks:

VARIABLE LENGTH? (Y OR N) <u>Y</u>

We answer yes. (We will not explain this feature here.)

Next, the program asks us to specify the action to be taken:

ENTER FUNCTION (A, C, D, E, S OR STOP) <u>A</u>

The command A is used to add new names to the list. On a standard diskette we can store more than 1,000 names this way. The other available choices are:

C can be used to change an entry in the list.

D can be used to delete an entry from the list.

E can be used to examine one or more entries in that list.

S can be used to save what has been typed onto the disk.

STOP can be used to stop the NADENTRY program.

We will now enter a complete name and address:

RECORD NUMBER IS 1

ENTER NAME (30) TOM BROWN

ENTER LINE ONE OF ADDRESS (30) SYBEX

ENTER LINE TWO OF ADDRESS (30) 2344 SIXTH ST

ENTER CITY (24) BERKELEY

ENTER STATE CA

ENTER ZIP (5) 94710

ENTER PHONE 415 848 8233

The numbers in parentheses indicate the maximum number of characters that may be used. We are now requested to specify which reference field we intend to use to selectively retrieve names from our file:

ENTER REFERENCE M-32-GR-180

We will use the reference field as follows:

— The first letter in the field specifies whether the person is male or female.

— The second group of two digits specifies the age of the person (in this case, 32).

— The next field specifies the color of the eyes (in this case, green)

— The last field specifies the weight of the person in pounds (in this case, 180).

The dashes between the numbers are not required but improve the readability of the program. Naturally, other data could also have been used in that reference field.

Let us now add four more names:

ENTER FUNCTION (A, C, D, E, S OR STOP) A

RECORD NUMBER IS 2

ENTER NAME (30) NANCY BLUE

ENTER LINE ONE OF ADDRESS (30) DOCTORS INC

ENTER LINE TWO OF ADDRESS (30) 33 CEDAR ST

ENTER CITY (24) BERKELEY

(Reset entry)

ENTER STATE CA

ENTER ZIP (5) 94709

ENTER PHONE 415 524 1234

ENTER REFERENCE F-20-BR-163

ENTER FUNCTION (A, C, D, E, S OR STOP) A   (Add one more)

RECORD NUMBER IS 3

ENTER NAME (30) BARBARA RED

ENTER LINE ONE OF ADDRESS (30) 10 GREEN ST

ENTER LINE TWO OF ADDRESS (30)

ENTER CITY (24) ALBANY

(Reset entry)

ENTER STATE CA

ENTER ZIP (5) 94000

ENTER PHONE 415 233 2909

ENTER REFERENCE F-29-BL-169 }   (Reset entry continued)

ENTER FUNCTION (A, C, D, E, S, OR STOP) A

RECORD NUMBER IS 4

ENTER NAME (30) JIM BROWN

ENTER LINE ONE OF ADDRESS (30) 55 AVOCADO ST

ENTER LINE TWO OF ADDRESS (30)

ENTER CITY (24) RICHMOND

ENTER STATE CA   (Next entry)

ENTER ZIP (5) 93333

ENTER PHONE 415 434 4533

ENTER REFERENCE M-44-BK-170

ENTER FUNCTION (A, C, D, E, S OR STOP) A

RECORD NUMBER IS 5

ENTER NAME (30) HENRY FOURTH

ENTER LINE ONE OF ADDRESS (30) KINGDOM INC.

ENTER LINE TWO OF ADDRESS (30) MAIDEN LANE

ENTER CITY (24) SAN FRANCISCO   (Next entry)

ENTER STATE CA

ENTER ZIP (5) 94121

ENTER PHONE 415 211 0298

ENTER REFERENCE M-51-GY-173

We have now typed five names and addresses. Let us verify that they are spelled correctly. We will use the EXAMINE command:

ENTER FUNCTION (A, C, D, E, S OR STOP) E

EXAMINE 1,5

By typing 1,5, we specify that records 1 through 5 should be displayed:

1   TOM BROWN
    SYBEX
    2344 SIXTH ST
    BERKELEY CA 94710 415 848 8233
    M-32-GR-180

2   NANCY BLUE
    DOCTORS INC
    33 CEDAR ST
    BERKELEY CA 94709 415 524 1234
    F-20-BR-163

3   BARBARA RED
    10 GREEN ST

    ALBANY CA 94000 415 233 2909
    F-29-BL-169

4   JIM BROWN
    55 AVOCADO ST

    RICHMOND CA 93333 415 434 4533
    M-44-BK-170

5   HENRY FOURTH
    KINGDOM INC.
    MAIDEN LANE
    SAN FRANCISCO CA 94121 415 211 0298
    M-51-GY-173

In order to stop the examination, we now type:

ESC   (A special key on the keyboard)

Since our five names and addresses are correct, we are done. If they had not been correct, we could have changed any line by using the "C" command. Let us save our entries on the disk.

Remember that with most programs, anything that is typed goes into the computer's memory, which is volatile. If you should leave the computer or turn it off at this point, your information may be lost. Therefore, it is necessary to explicitly save the information onto the disk. This is the purpose of the S (SAVE) command. Use this command frequently to avoid the risk of losing information that has been typed. Let us save records 1 through 5:

ENTER FUNCTION (A, C, D, E, S OR STOP) <u>S</u>

NUMBER OF NAD RECORDS SAVED: 5

The program confirms that five records (names and addresses) have been saved on the disk now.

We are done. Let us leave the entry program:

ENTER FUNCTION (A, C, D, E, S OR STOP) <u>STOP</u>

NADENTRY COMPLETED

We will now print our list, sort it and select entries. In order to print it, we will use another module of the NAD set of programs called NADPRINT. Then, instead of doing a straight listing, we will perform a selection.

The "menu" is displayed again on the screen:

1	CREATE OR MODIFY A NAD FILE
2	EXTRACT NAMES FROM ONE FILE TO ANOTHER
3	PRINT A REPORT
4	PRINT MAILING LABELS
5	SORT BY LAST NAME
6	SORT BY ZIP CODE

7	CREATE NAME SRT FILE
8	CREATE ZIP SRT FILE
9	CHANGE SYSTEM DATE
ESC	STOP PROGRAM
CR	REFRESH MENU

ENTER NUMBER OF FUNCTION DESIRED 3

This time, we type "3". The program requests the name of the file
to be printed and the disk drive where it is located. Then it asks whether
we want to select names. We do not:

NADPRINT

ENTER FILE NAME MAILIST

ENTER DRIVE (A OR B) B

DO YOU WANT TO SELECT RECORDS (Y OR N)? N

(This listing is typed on the printer)

FILE: @:MAILIST.NAD		NAD—NAME AND ADDRESS SYSTEM				PAGE: 1
		NAD FILE PRINT				DATE: 04/18/80
RECORD					ZIP	
NUMBER	NAME	ADDRESS	CITY	STATE	CODE	PHONE NUMBER
1	TOM BROWN	SYBEX	2344 SIXTH ST	BERKELEY	CA	94710	415 848 8233
M-32-GR-180						
2	NANCY BLUE	DOCTORS INC	33 CEDAR ST	BERKELEY	CA	94709	415 524 12 34
F-20-BR - 163						
3	BARBARA RED	10 GREEN ST		ALBANY	CA	94000	415 233 2909
F-29-BL - 169						
4	JIM BROWN	55 AVOCADO ST		RICHMOND	CA	93333	415 434 4533
M-44-BK- 170						
5	HENRY FOURTH	KINGDOM INC.	MAIDEN LANE	SAN FRANCISCO	CA	94121	415 211 0298
M-51-GY-173						

PRINT FINISHED

THERE WERE 5 RECORDS WRITTEN

We can verify that our list is intact and correct. Let us now perform a selection.

The menu appears again, and we type "3". This time, however, we specify that a selection must be performed from the very first name (record #1). Next, we specify that the selection be performed from the contents of the reference field (REF).

NADPRINT

ENTER FILE NAME MAILIST

ENTER DRIVE (A OR B) B

DO YOU WANT TO SELECT RECORDS (Y OR N)? Y
ENTER STARTING RECORD NUMBER 1
ENTER NAME OF SELECTION FIELD REF

We can specify a "range" or a "match" when looking for a value in the reference field.

Here we specify a match. In other words, we will look for all names which have a specific letter in their reference field. In this case we will select all males, i.e., all persons who have M in location 1 of the REF field.

RANGE OR MATCH (R OR M)? M

ENTER MATCHING PATTERN M
DO YOU WANT UPPER CASE TRANSLATION (Y, N)? Y
ENTER FIRST STARTING LOCATION 1
ENTER LAST STARTING LOCATION 1

ALIGN FORMS IN PRINTER, THEN TYPE RETURN TO CONTINUE

The program executes and types the following:

RECORD NUMBER	NAME	ADDRESS		CITY	STATE	ZIP CODE	PAGE 1 PHONE NUMBER
1	TOM BROWN	SYBEX	2344 SIXTH ST	BERKELEY	CA	94710	415 848-8233
M-32-GR-180							
4	JIM BROWN	55 AVOCADO ST		RICHMOND	CA	93333	415 434 4533
M-44-BK-170							
5	HENRY FOURTH	KINGDOM INC.	MAIDEN LANE	SAN FRANCSICO	CA	94121	415 211 0298
M-51-GY-173							

PRINT FINISHED

THERE WERE 3 RECORDS WRITTEN

We have successfully selected all three male persons from our files! Just to make sure, let us now select the two female persons. The menu appears, we type "3", and go through a similar sequence:

NADPRINT

ENTER FILE NAME MAILIST

ENTER DRIVE (A OR B) B

DO YOU WANT TO SELECT RECORDS (Y OR N)? Y
ENTER STARTING RECORD NUMBER 1
ENTER NAME OF SELECTION FIELD REF
RANGE OR MATCH (R OR M)? M

ENTER MATCHING PATTERN F
DO YOU WANT UPPER CASE TRANSLATION (Y, N)? Y
ENTER FIRST STARTING LOCATION 1
ENTER LAST STARTING LOCATION 1

ALIGN FORMS IN PRINTER, THEN TYPE RETURN TO CONTINUE

```
              NAME AND ADDRESS PRINT FILE B:MAILIST.NAD

RECORD                                               ZIP      PAGE   1
NUMBER    NAME            ADDRESS         CITY    STATE  CODE PHONE NUMBER

   2    NANCY BLUE    DOCTORS INC  33 CEDAR ST  BERKELEY   CA   94709    415 524 1234
F-20-BR-163


   3    BARBARA RED   10 GREEN ST              ALBANY     CA   94000    415 233 2909
F-29-BL-169
```

PRINT FINISHED

THERE WERE 2 RECORDS WRITTEN

The sequence is the same as before except this time we specify a matching pattern "F". You can verify that we have successfully retrieved the two female persons from our five-name list.

Let us perform one more selection to demonstrate the power of this selection mechanism: we will now retrieve all persons living in Berkeley. Instead of using the REF field, this time we will use the city field:

NADPRINT

ENTER FILE NAME MAILIST

ENTER DRIVE (A OR B) B

DO YOU WANT TO SELECT RECORDS (Y OR N)? Y
ENTER STARTING RECORD NUMBER 1
ENTER NAME OF SELECTION FIELD CITY
RANGE OR MATCH (R OR M)? M

ENTER MATCHING PATTERN BERKELEY
DO YOU WANT UPPER CASE TRANSLATION (Y, N)? Y
ENTER FIRST STARTING LOCATION 1
ENTER LAST STARTING LOCATION 1

ALIGN FORMS IN PRINTER, THEN TYPE RETURN TO CONTINUE

```
              NAME AND ADDRESS PRINT FILE B:MAILIST.NAD

RECORD                                                    ZIP
NUMBER    NAME              ADDRESS        CITY    STATE  CODE  PHONE NUMBER

   1    TOM BROWN     SYBEX       2344 SIXTH ST  BERKELEY    CA    94710    415 848 8233
M-32-GR-180

   2    NANCY BLUE    DOCTORS INC  33 CEDAR ST   BERKELEY    CA    94709    415 524 1234
F-20-BR-163
```

PRINT FINISHED

THERE WERE 2 RECORDS WRITTEN

Sorting

We will now sort our list in function of various criteria. First, let us sort it by ZIP. The sequence below is self-explanatory:

ENTER NUMBER OF FUNCTION DESIRED <u>8</u>

ENTER NAME OF FILE TO BE SORTED (1-8 CHARS) <u>MAILIST</u>

ENTER INPUT FILE DRIVE (@,A-F:RET=CURLOG) <u>A</u>

ENTER NAME OF SORTED OUTPUT FILE (1-8 CHARS) <u>ZIPLIST</u>

ENTER SORTED OUTPUT FILE DRIVE (@,A-F:RET=CURLOG) <u>A</u>

ENTER LENGTH OF NAD FILE REFERENCE FIELD (0-127) <u>20</u>

ZIP SORT PARAMETER FILE CREATED

The menu appears again, and we type 6. (On the Cromemco computer, the command is different, and "QSORT ZIP" must be typed instead.)

In order to verify that the "sort" worked, let us list the resulting file.

120 YOUR FIRST COMPUTER

```
***********          N A D          ***********
              N A D   S Y S T E M   M E N U

   1     CREATE OR MODIFY A NAD FILE

   2     EXTRACT NAMES FROM ONE FILE TO ANOTHER

   3     PRINT A REPORT

   4     PRINT MAILING LABELS

   5     SORT BY LAST NAME

   6     SORT BY ZIP CODE

   7     CREATE NAME SRT FILE

   8     CREATE ZIP SRT FILE

   9     CHANGE SYSTEM DATE

   ESC        STOP PROGRAM

   CR         REFRESH MENU
```

ENTER NUMBER OF FUNCTION DESIRED 3

NADPRINT

ENTER FILE NAME ZIPLIST

ENTER DRIVE (A OR B) A

DO YOU WANT TO SELECT RECORDS (Y OR N)? N

NAD—NAME AND ADDRESS SYSTEM

NAD FILE PRINT

RECORD NUMBER	NAME	ADDRESS		CITY	STATE	ZIP CODE	PHONE NUMBER
1	JIM BROWN	55 AVOCADO ST		RICHMOND	CA	93333	415 434 4533
M-44-BK-170							
2	BARBARA RED	10 GREEN ST		ALBANY	CA	94000	415 233 2909
F-29-BL-169							
3	HENRY FOURTH	KINGDOM INC.	MAIDEN LANE	SAN FRANCISCO	CA	94121	415 211 0298
M-51-GY-173							
4	NANCY BLUE	DOCTORS INC	33 CEDAR ST	BERKELEY	CA	94709	415 524 1234
F-20-BR-163							
5	TOM BROWN	SYBEX	2344 SIXTH ST	BERKELEY	CA	94710	415 848 8233
M-32-GR-180							

PRINT FINISHED

THERE WERE 5 RECORDS WRITTEN

PRINT ANOTHER NAD FILE? (Y, N) N

It worked.

We could also have sorted the list in function of other criteria. For example, we could sort it by ascending names. This would be somewhat more complex, but it would serve to demonstrate the power of a sorting program such as QSORT.

QSORT needs a "parameter file" that specifies the standard sorting parameters, such as the name of the file to be sorted, the criterion used, etc. Let us create this parameter file. We will now execute the QPARM program in order to create the parameter file to be used by the sorting program. Let us execute it with the CRUN compiler. The complete dialogue appears:

A. CRUN QPARM

CRUN VER 2.04 K

ENTER PARAMETER FILE NAME ? AGE

ENTER INPUT FILE DRIVE ? B

ENTER INPUT FILE NAME ? MAILIST

ENTER INPUT FILE TYPE ? NAD

ENTER OUTPUT FILE DRIVE ? B

ENTER OUTPUT FILE NAME ? AGELIST

ENTER OUTPUT FILE TYPE ? NAD

ENTER LOGICAL RECORD LENGTH IN DECIMAL ? 148

WANT OUTPUT FILE BACKED UP ? Y

WANT TO CHANGE OUTPUT DISKETTE ? N

WANT CONSOLE OUTPUT ? Y

ENTER WORK FILE DRIVE ? B

The file containing the parameters is called AGE and resides on disk drive A. The file to be sorted is called MAILIST (of type NAD) and is stored in drive B. The sorted list that will be created is to be called AGELIST (of type NAD) and will be stored automatically on disk drive B. Since this system allows records of various lengths to be used, it is necessary to specify the record length used by the file. It should be noted that it is important to specify the record length and such other parameters. A mistake in specification will cause the sorting operation to fail. Computers require totally accurate commands.

The rest of the questions asked by the system are not important here. Standard answers are provided.

The actual selection specifications can now be entered:

ENTER KEY # 1 STARTING POSITION ? <u>128</u>
ENTER KEY # 1 LENGTH ? <u>2</u>
ENTER KEY # 1 ASCEND/DESCEND FLAG ? <u>A</u>
ENTER KEY # 1 ALPHA/NUMERIC FLAG ? <u>N</u>

ENTER KEY # 2 STARTING POSITION ? <u>0</u>
BUILDING PARAMETER RECORD

The selection will be performed by ascending ages. The age is specified in the third character position of the reference field. Within the record, the first character of the REF field is numbered as 126. Therefore, the age is stored at starting position 128 as specified above. Its length is two characters, and the sort will be performed in ascending order.

This program asks us whether we still want other parameters to be used in the sort. No other parameters are used here, so we type a 0. This stops the QPARM program and automatically builds the parameter list called AGE. AGE is now ready to use.

We use the QSORT program with the AGE parameter list:

A. <u>QSORT AGE</u>
QSORT VER:1.5
      INPUT RECORDS READ: 5
      WORKFILES USED: 0
      OUTPUT RECORDS WRITTEN: 5
      BYTES IN BUFFER: 51829
      BYTES PER LOGICAL RECORD: 148
      KEYS SPECIFIED: 1

SORT COMPLETED

Let us now print the sorted file with NAD:

ENTER FILE NAME <u>AGELIST</u>

ENTER DRIVE (A OR B) <u>B</u>

DO YOU WANT TO SELECT RECORDS (Y OR N) ? <u>N</u>

ALIGN FORMS IN PRINTER, THEN TYPE RETURN TO CONTINUE

```
                    NAME AND ADDRESS PRINT FILE B:AGELIST.NAD

RECORD
                                                              ZIP
NUMBER    NAME              ADDRESS         CITY      STATE  CODE  PHONE NUMBER

   1   NANCY BLUE      DOCTORS INC  33 CEDAR ST  BERKELEY     CA    94709   415 524 1234
F-20-BR-163


   2   BARBARA RED     10 GREEN ST               ALBANY       CA    94000   415 233 2909
F-29-BL-169


   3   TOM BROWN       SYBEX        2344 SIXTH ST  BERKELEY   CA    94710   415 848 8233
M-32-GR-180


   4   JIM BROWN       55 AVOCADO ST             RICHMOND     CA    93333   415 434 4533
M-44-BK-170


   5   HENRY FOURTH  KINGDOM INC.  MAIDEN LANE SAN FRANCISCO  CA    94121   415 211 0298
M-51-GY-173
```

PRINT FINISHED

THERE WERE 5 RECORDS WRITTEN

By examining the list above, you can verify that the names have, indeed, been sorted in order of ascending ages. We could have used another criterion and sorted them in alphabetical order by name, city, or even by telephone number. We could also have used the LABEL option. This would automatically print the names and addresses on labels. In fact, there are even more complex selection operations that could have been performed.

Mailing List Summary

The previous example shows how simple it is to use a mailing list program. Information can be coded in the reference field, then used to retrieve names selectively. This is a powerful aid that can be used for sales, marketing and any applications that may require sorting or retrieval. For example, the index of this book was created with the NAD program. Index words were entered as names, the rest of the address field was left blank, and the page number was entered as part of the REF field. The words for the index were entered in random order, and then sorted alphabetically. Similar creative applications are possible with any powerful mailing list program.

A Word Processing Program

We will now show how easy it is to use one of the CP/M-compatible word processing programs available today. Technically, a word processing program combines an *editor* program (for entering text) with a *formatting* program (for printing text). Basically, a word processor is a program designed so that text can be conveniently typed on the screen, edited and modified and then printed in an easy-to-read format. Word processors are now extensively used in businesses to type correspondence, manuals and even books.

A rough draft is first typed on the terminal and then corrected by the typist. Next, a printout is generated. The person who originally composed the letter or the text then inspects the printout and indicates changes that should be performed. The text is edited on the screen until it reaches final form. A perfect, corrected text is then printed. A number of different formatting options may be used during the printing. The text can be left-justified, right-justified, and tabulated, for example.

A word processor is often used for contracts and other business documents where a few words have to be frequently inserted while the bulk of the text is left unchanged. A perfect printout can be obtained every time with minimal effort.

For this example, we will use an actual word processor program called "WordStar" (designed and trademarked by MicroPro International, San Rafael, California). This program is available on diskette under the name WM. Let us call it:

A. <u>WM</u>

A menu immediately appears on the screen:

```
D = EDIT A DOCUMENT FILE
N = EDIT A NON-DOCUMENT FILE
X = EXIT TO OPERATING SYSTEM
H = SET HELP LEVEL
P = PRINT A FILE
K = DELETE A FILE
```

Six commands are available. We type "D" as we wish to edit a document file. A new menu appears on the screen:

NAME OF FILE TO EDIT (OR RETURN)?

We are requested to specify the name of the file that we want to create. We will call it LETTER:

NAME OF FILE TO EDIT (OR RETURN)? LETTER

We terminate our entry with a return, and the following menu appears on the screen:

```
        PAGE 1 LINE 14 COL 01              INSERT ON
CURSOR:    ^A = left word       ^S = left char       ^D = right char     ^F = right word
           ^E = up line         ^X = down line
SCROLL:    ^Z = up line         ^W = down line       ^C = up screen      ^R = down screen
DELETE:    DEL = char left      ^G = char right      ^T = word right     ^Y = entire line
OTHER:     ^V = insert on/off   ^I = tab             RETURN = end para   ^U = stop
           ^N = insert a RETURN ^B = reform to end para                  ^L = find/replace again
HELP:      ^J displays menu of information commands
PREFIX KEYS    ^Q  ^J  ^K  ^O  ^P     display menus of additional commands
L----|----|----|----|----|----|----|----|----|----|----|--------R
```

This menu summarizes the commands available to edit the text. Six categories of commands are provided. We will explain them briefly here.

—The CURSOR COMMANDS will move the cursor on the screen. The cursor appears on our display as a triangle that always points to a specific location on the screen. Normally, this is the location where the next letter typed will be placed. We need to be able to move this cursor up, down, left and right. The cursor commands allow us to do so.

All of the command letters on the screen are preceded by a ^ sign. This symbol is used to represent a control character. For example, ^ A means that the control key must be held depressed while the character A is pressed. This will result in the cursor being moved to the beginning of the word on its left.

—SCROLL COMMANDS: After we have typed a few lines of text, the screen will begin to fill up. As we continue typing, the lines at the top of the screen will move up automatically, and the top line of the text will disappear from the screen when the screen is full. The line that disappears from the top of the screen is not lost; it is stored in the computer's memory. Because of the limited size of the screen, however, only part of the text can be displayed at any time. If we wish to examine the top or bottom of the text, we will have to make the lines move up and down on our screen. This is called scrolling.

—DELETE FACILITIES are self explanatory.

—The control characters, listed under the category OTHER, vary in function. For example, ^ V will be used to insert additional text in the middle of a line. It will be used in our example. We will press ^ V in order to turn the insert mode on, and press ^ V again to turn this mode off.

After performing various insertions, our text will be jagged. In order to have it justified left and right, we would use ^ B to align it. In addition, if we were looking for specific words in the text, we would use ^ L to locate them. A powerful editor allows us to find any occurrence of any string of characters in the text and substitute another one for it automatically.

—The HELP command displays the menu of the commands available.

—The PREFIX control characters display menus of additional commands for accomplishing specific functions. They are used to format the output, print, etc. We will not use them here.

Let us now type in a business letter. As we type, the cursor automatically moves to the next character on the right. Notice what is happening on the screen:

April 16, 1980

ABC Company
12 Third Street
Berkeley, California 94710

Dear Customer:

This is to let you know that our new model is now available. I have enclosed a catalog with an order form for your conv ▲

We finish typing the word convenience, and the characters "conv" are automatically removed from one line and moved to the next. The first line is also automatically expanded to the width of our screen. The program provides automatic left and right justification:

April 16, 1980

ABC Company
12 Third Street
Berkeley, California 94711

Dear Customer:

This is to let you know that our new model is now available. I have enclosed a catalog with an order form for your convenience ▲

Let us now finish our letter:

Dear Customer:

This is to let you know that our new model is now available. I have enclosed a catalog with an order form for your convenience. Supply is limited. Order now.

Sincerely yours,

Mary
Customer Service ▲

Notice how the top lines of the letter have "fallen off" the top of the screen with the automatic scrolling feature.

Let us now add an extra sentence to our letter. We will move the cursor up by using ⌃ E (refer to the cursor commands at the top of the screen). We will then position it to the left of the screen by pressing as many ⌃ S's as necessary. Once we reach the left of the line, above "Sincerely yours", we turn the insert mode on by pushing ⌃ V (refer to OTHER in the list of control characters on the menu). The screen now appears as follows:

```
^K                PAGE 1 LINE 15 COL 01          INSERT ON

      ^K PREFIX                    (to cancel prefix, hit SPACE bar)
END EDIT/SAVE:     D = Done edit   X = done, eXit   S = Save, reedit   Q = abandon
MARK BLOCK:        B = Block start  K = block end    H = Hide/display
BLOCK OPERATIONS:  B = moVe block  C = Copy block   Y = delete block  W = Write
ADDITIONAL FILES:  R = Read file    W = Write block  J = delete file
PLACE MARKERS:     0-9 = set/hide place marker 0-9
PRINTING:          P = Print a file




Dear Customer:

This is to let you know that our new model is now available.
I have enclosed a catalog with an order form for your
convenience. Supply is limited. Order now.
▲
Sincerely yours,

Mary
Customer Service
```

Notice that "Insert On" now appears at the very top of the screen.
This alerts us to the fact that whatever we type will be added to the text
rather than superimposed on top of it. We then add an extra line of text:

```
Dear Customer:

This is to let you know that our new model is now available.
I have enclosed a catalog with an order form for your
convenience. Supply is limited. Order now.

A special discount of 10 percent applies to orders received
within 10 days!
▲
Sincerely yours,

Mary
Customer Service
```

We turn the insert mode off by hitting ^ V. It is that simple! If we want to change a character, we simply position the cursor on top of it and retype the correct character. If we want to erase a word and replace it with another one, we position the cursor and use the command ^ T to erase the word, then we use the ^ V command to insert a new one. We can insert a word or a whole sentence if we so desire. After we are finished with all of the changes, we can use the ^ B command to realign all of the lines correctly.

Once we are satisfied with the appearance of the letter, we will save it on a disk, and then print it. We type ^ K and another menu appears on the screen:

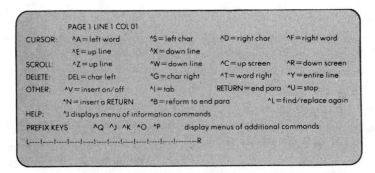

We now type D (done edit), and the system confirms this by displaying the following on the screen:

SAVING FILE LETTER

Our file LETTER is now saved on the disk. The original menu appears again:

```
NO FILE IS NOW BEING EDITED

D = EDIT A DOCUMENT FILE
N = EDIT A NON-DOCUMENT FILE
X = EXIT TO OPERATING SYSTEM
H = SET HELP LEVEL
P = PRINT A FILE
K = DELETE A FILE
```

We respond with a P and a new menu is displayed:

P NO FILE IS NOW BEING EDITED

NAME OF FILE TO PRINT? <u>LETTER</u>

FOR DEFAULT HIT RETURN FOR EACH QUESTION:
  DISK FILE OUTPUT (Y, N): <u>N</u>
  START AT PAGE NUMBER (RETURN FOR BEGINNING)?
  USE FORM FEEDS (Y, N): <u>N</u>
  SUPPRESS PAGE FORMATTING (Y, N): <u>N</u>
  PAUSE FOR PAPER CHANGE BETWEEN PAGES (Y, N): <u>N</u>
READY PRINTER, HIT RETURN:

Once we have answered the various questions, the letter is automatically typed on the printer. It is now perfect, but if we do not like it, we can easily use the word processing program again to modify it.

Summary of Word Processing Program

This example showed how easy it is to use a word processor and how powerful this program can be. The program is equipped with several other features that provide convenient and powerful options for transforming the text. For example, parts of different letters can be conveniently merged together. Words or even sentences can be automatically substituted. The letter which we have designated could even be coupled with the mailing list program, so that personalized letters could be sent to all the names on our mailing list. Applications are limited only by your imagination.

Summary

Two typical business programs have been described in a realistic environment. They should give you a feeling for the steps involved in using such programs, as well as the benefits of these particular application programs.

We will now review the two limiting constraints on small computers: hardware and software.

THE HARDWARE CONSTRAINTS

The hardware components of a system have been examined systematically in the previous chapters. The essential considerations will be summarized here. The speed of the processor is seldom a consideration for the majority of business applications. The amount of memory required by most business programs is 48K to 64K. Limited applications can operate on less memory.

Disks usually impose the greatest limitation. Two full-size (8-inch) diskettes are required for most applications. For larger files, a hard disk (or several hard disks) are highly desirable. Winchester disks offer large storage capacity, and are faster than floppy disks. However, they are generally slower than traditional hard disks. Such a traditional hard disk may be advisable, despite its higher cost, in the case of business applications that require a great deal of file-handling. A hard disk also requires back-up storage. This back-up is usually in the form of a removable cartridge or a magnetic tape.

When a system is utilized by several users simultaneously (through time-sharing), a hard disk is practically indispensable. Multiple disk units are required if several large files must be accessible on-line.

Two main types of printers may be considered for business purposes:
— A daisy wheel printer for automated business letters and high-quality printouts
— A line printer for speed.
Both types of printers may be required. In the case of large files, however, the line printer is recommended.

In summary, there are no longer any significant hardware constraints when selecting the components of a business system. Let us examine the software constraints.

SOFTWARE CONSTRAINTS

Most microcomputer systems available today offer the hardware capabilities required to perform all of the operations that have been described at a sufficient speed, provided no complex arithmetic is required. Unfortunately, many business programs have been developed that do not totally automate all of the tasks required. We can easily see, from the above description, that the task of the file management system and the various processing programs is complex. In the past, because of the high cost, such programs have been created only for larger computers. The cost of developing such programs is now much larger than the cost of the actual hardware on which it resides. For this reason, manufacturers in the business of selling hardware are usually not anxious to develop such expensive programs. Consulting firms and software houses have traditionally maintained a good business selling specialized programs or packages to business users. However, because software cannot be efficiently protected against duplication, it is difficult to sell software programs for low-cost hardware at a profit. This has slowed down software development.

Most microcomputer systems available today offer a number of business packages that were originally developed by software companies. These packages are generally designed to operate on a minimum system, and, as a result, are usually independent programs.

For example, there is an accounts receivable program, an accounts payable program, and an inventory program, etc. These separate "packages" are used to maintain independent files. If the number of transactions are high for any one of these files, they provide a valuable service. However, they perform only part of the job. The business user is still required to manually update all of the files that might be involved in a single transaction.

When selecting software, it is, therefore, important to remember that most packages operate independently. A superior software system automates everything and requires minimal operator intervention. However, it may require one or more hard disks.

CP/M, a standard operating system, is now widely used. Programs designed to run under CP/M become computer-independent. A number of different vendors provide powerful software packages, including languages (BASIC, PASCAL, FORTRAN, COBOL, etc.) that can run under CP/M. This is a significant advantage for business users.

When selecting a system, it is important to examine the available software, and to determine whether such software will do the job. It is generally not easy to convert to a new program, and the first choice should be a good one. Systems that support CP/M offer the advantage of a wide software selection.

USING MICROCOMPUTERS FOR BUSINESS APPLICATIONS

Now that the limitations have been pointed out, let us discuss some of the positive aspects of using a microcomputer system in a business application. The facilities that have been described are ideal for a business automation system. However, even solutions far from this ideal will provide benefits in excess of the cost of the system. A useful system can be purchased for as little as $5,000 to $10,000, which with minimal software packages will permit the automation of the inventory, the accounts payable, the accounts receivable, and often other functions such as mailing lists, back-orders, payroll or tax computations. The benefits obtained from automation will almost always far outweigh the initial cost of the system. For this reason, microcomputer systems are a very valuable tool even for limited business automation.

Bear in mind, however, that an invisible price will be paid. If extensive files are created, or if specific programs are written, the software investment will become dominant. After a period of time, the investment needed to structure these files or develop new programs will become much more significant than the initial purchase price of the system. And, after a few years, limitations may be felt and a larger, more complete system may be desired. Of course, there is a possibility that the manufacturer of the original system will have expanded the system's resources. However, this is usually unlikely in the long run. In view of the constantly decreasing price of hardware, it is more likely that, within a few years, the hardware itself will be obsolete, and the manufacturer will be marketing a new system, which will not be completely compatible with the first one. The business user will then have to move to the new system and reformat his/her files or use different programs.

However, even if the first system is essentially abandoned after a few years, it will have provided an extremely valuable transition into the computerized business management world. While the initial hardware investment will have been lost after a few years, and a substantial software investment might also be lost, these initial investments will have been translated into a structuring of business procedures, computerized operation, the training of personnel, and an awareness by management of the additional capabilities that will be needed in future systems. Such a system will provide immediate initial benefits that will far outweigh its cost, and will provide substantial educational benefits to its purchaser. After using such a system for one or two years, the intelligent purchaser who understands the nature of his/her needs will be in a position to thoroughly understand the ideal system required to fulfill these needs. At this point, the second choice is likely to be an optimal one.

The comparison is analogous to the recommendation that a new driver should first drive a low-cost car before purchasing the car of his/her dreams. The first machine may be inadequate, but it provides educational value by expanding the skills of its user.

WHAT ABOUT MINICOMPUTERS?

Larger, more powerful, and expensive minicomputers might appear, at first, to provide an answer to the general-purpose business management capability. This is not necessarily true. Perhaps 90% of all mini-computers are used for applications other than business. Most minis are used for industrial automation and specialized data acquisition. Only about 10% are used in business applications. The reason is again the same: manufacturers sell hardware and are not anxious to develop extremely costly software packages on which they cannot realize a substantial profit. As a result, few general-purpose business programs have been made available. The best systems for business applications, i.e., those that incorporate a maximum of automated software facilities, are the large computer systems that sell for hundreds of thousands of dollars. On such costly computers, it is reasonable to install expensive software.

However, one of the parameters of the equation has changed. The availability of very low cost microcomputer systems means that, for the first time, there is the possibility of selling software that can be amortized over a large number of units. For this reason, a majority of the highly complex programs previously available only on large scale computers will probably become available on microcomputers. We can predict that, within a few years, microcomputers will become powerful business tools equipped with a majority of the functions required for efficient business management. The systems that are available today are the first step in that direction.

CUSTOM BUSINESS PROGRAMS

Once the specific needs of a business have been identified, the potential buyer is then able to evaluate whether a specific micro-computer system will meet those needs. If the system does not, then additional software programs or packages should be obtained. The essential questions, at this point are: is it worth writing a program yourself, or is it worth contracting outside help in order to add specific programs required by the business? The usual answer to both questions is no. However, if the programming capabilities are available in-house, or if the educational value of programming is significant to you, then it might be worthwhile to write your own programs. The important point is that most business users simply underestimate the amount of effort needed for a usable, correct, and documented business program. While a program in a high-level language such as BASIC can be quickly developed that will appear to meet specific needs, unless such a program is well-written, well-documented, and adaptable to the needs of the business and the existing system, it might do more harm than good. A file management program may become essentially useless after a certain number of items have been entered, because its efficiency breaks down, or because it is incapable of managing certain items. Additional failures, which no one in the company may be able to correct, may occur when certain types of data are entered or used.

Creating a complete, debugged, usable system is typically a long and expensive task. Programs that have been in existence for some time and have been tested on other users are the most desirable programs to obtain. In addition, a system should be integrated, from a software standpoint; all programs should be capable of handling common file structures, and updating the required files. Programs simply added on to a system might not be able to make use of its facilities, or might create structures that other programs will not be able to use.

However, packaged programs might not be optimal for your specific business. In this case, you will have to evaluate a trade-off between:
- Packaged programs that can be modified or adapted, preferably by an in-house programmer. This will result in a better efficiency of the programs for your specific business procedures or requirements.
- Customizing, or adding programs that will increase the overall cost of the system, and may detract from its reliability.

In general, the use of packaged programs is highly recommended. You may have to adapt a few procedures, but the program will do the job reliably and economically.

STANDARD SOFTWARE

Most microcomputer systems today are available with simple business packages. These programs are designed to automate transactions. Any business with a large number of repetitive transactions will accrue benefits from computer automation.

However, this is true only if the type of "standard package" available with the system fits the business. For example, a sales entry program might ask so many questions that it would require twice as much time as manual processing. In such a case, the automation is worthwhile only if additional benefits accrue. Such additional benefits are: data entry discipline enforcements, automatic processing or updating of other files, and report generation.

If these additional programs or benefits exist, then even a somewhat cumbersome, "standardized" data entry program will still yield benefits. *Caution:* if these additional facilities do not yet exist on the system that you are considering, then you should evaluate the advantages and disadvantages carefully. Many small businesses find manual order processing or bookkeeping more practical and economical than a "standard" business package.

If a part-time programmer is available, or can be justified, many special-purpose programs can be developed that conform to the needs of a business. If the programmer is good, all potential benefits of a computer system will accrue, resulting in a number of improvements that have been described previously: efficiency, lower cost, increased reliability, instantaneous management information, improved collecting of receivables, automation of new business procedures (automatic reorder, credit check, and specialized mailings).

Microcomputers available today offer all of the required hardware resources at low cost. Software, however, often makes the difference between a good and bad investment in a system.

In order to facilitate a choice, a minimal checklist of required facilities is shown.

REQUIRED BUSINESS FACILITIES
A SOFTWARE CHECKLIST

1. LISTS
- ☐ Customers
- ☐ Suppliers
- ☐ Inventory
- ☐ Orders
- ☐ Salesmen
- ☐ Packing list
- ☐ Shipping list
- ☐ Employees

2. JOURNALS
- ☐ Payments received
- ☐ General ledger
- ☐ Account receivable
- ☐ Accounts payable
- ☐ Bank accounts
- ☐ Tax records

3. BUSINESS FORMS
- ☐ Invoices
- ☐ Labels
- ☐ Checks
- ☐ Payroll
- ☐ Form letters
- ☐ Statements
- ☐ Special notices
- ☐ Tax reports

4. REPORTS
- ☐ Past-due accounts
- ☐ Sales reports
- ☐ Inventory reports (aged, per category, per item, etc.)
- ☐ Back orders
- ☐ Aged accounts (receivable, payable)
- ☐ Sorted mailing list
- ☐ Customer sales record
- ☐ All files sorted per a specific criterion
- ☐ Salesmen commissions and performance
- ☐ Employees overtime, vacation, sick-leave

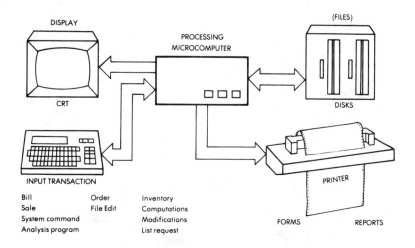

Figure 7-11:   The elements of a business system

SUMMARY

Using small computers for business applications requires specific hardware and software capabilities. Software capabilities have been described in this chapter and illustrated by typical business programs such as a mailing list and a word processor.

The new mass market created by microcomputers has resulted in the availability of low-cost software modules. These standard packages make business automation available to any business. Their advantages and limitations have been described.

When buying a system, the following steps should be considered:

1. There must be a need. The nature and amount of work must justify a change. This can be measured by the number of identical transactions or reports to be generated. In addition, the computer system may often be justified by the unique problems it may solve in special situations, such as inventory management, mailing list, management reports.

2. When to buy? Prices for electronics continue to decrease every year, while prices for peripherals tend to stabilize, or decrease slowly. Therefore, tomorrow's system will always be cheaper than today's. However, a computer system means savings of N dollars per month. Deferring its installation by m months is equivalent to a loss of m × N dollars.

3. Which system to buy? The main options and equipment available will be presented in the next chapter.

8

SELECTING A SYSTEM

INTRODUCTION

The selection of a microcomputer system can be guided by the same general principles as the selection of any highly complex system. Numerous trade-offs exist, which result in a wide array of performance and convenience advantages and disadvantages. To make a reasonable choice, the user should first define (and understand) his/her main goals. Once these essential goals are set, the user can then evaluate the criteria for selection knowledgeably.

Users can be unrealistic when selecting a microcomputer system; they often expect their system to be best at any operation (as well as inexpensive). The first section of this chapter describes the criteria usually employed in evaluating the different systems. The second section uses these criteria to analyze which types of systems are best suited for specific classes of applications. An overview of the major existing commercial systems will be presented in Chapter 10.

CRITERIA FOR SELECTION

The main criteria used when selecting a microcomputer are usually: low cost, performance, complete hardware, complete software, convenience and reliability. Let us now describe each of these criteria.

Low Cost

From a general standpoint, pricing among the various manufacturers is so competitive that virtually all equivalent systems sell at a similar price. A low price can therefore not be applied as a criterion for selecting a specific manufacturer, but tends to be generally representative of a smaller set of components or facilities for a given system. Of course, price wars may make one particular system more attractive for a limited period of time.

As a general rule, the user interested in the lowest possible cost should first look at a single board. For less then $250 he/she will be able to acquire a minimal microprocessor system that will require an extra power supply (which costs approximately $50). The user will then be able to communicate in hexadecimal. If, however, the user's ambitions are somewhat higher and he/she wishes to do actual programming, then a system should be purchased that, at a minimum includes the following: a PC board with at least 4K of RAM, an enclosure, a power supply, an alphanumeric keyboard, a CRT display for output, and a tape cassette (as a mass storage medium).

However, it must be stressed that if the user wants a more complete system, the cost of the CPU board itself is no longer the dominant cost in the complete system. (This has always been true, until very recently, in the history of computers.) The main cost of a system is now that of the peripherals. A good printer alone will be more expensive than the CPU. In addition, the overall value and cost of the system cannot be measured in hardware terms alone. The software is usually an expensive resource in any system.

For this reason, it can be argued that independent of other criteria (except in the case of a truly minimal expenditure), the actual cost of the microcomputer box is not a relevant criterion for selection.

Price Evolution

Prices will decrease every year for virtually all electronic elements of a system. This has been true of computers in the past, and, as yet, a price limit has not been reached. However, the cost of peripherals may not decrease as significantly.

After the choice of a system has been made, and the system delivered, there will probably be a lower cost option made available for at least one of the elements of the system.

This does not mean that you should wait for the lowest possible price. Make the best choice now, and start using your system. The enjoyment of a personal computer, or the benefits of a business system begin to accrue immediately, and are much more satisfactory than the savings obtained by waiting.

The knowledge that you will gain by using a computer system will also prove beneficial to your professional life, as well as to your ability to select other systems in the future. In short, once the overall price level has been determined to be acceptable, don't waste time trimming off 10 or 20 per cent.

Performance

The word performance, when used to describe a system, can often be misleading. Let us first look at the *hardware performance* of a system, which is often measured by the speed of the CPU. The speed of the CPU must be sufficiently matched by a low access time of the memory, so that the MPU never has to wait for data. However, if one microcomputer has a 2MHz (megahertz) clock rate, and another microcomputer has a 4MHz rate, this does not necessarily mean that one processor is twice as fast as the other. There is simply no obvious relationship between the clock rate and the actual speed at which instructions are executed.

The *clock rate* is the rate at which pulses must be transmitted to the MPU chip so that it can properly execute instructions. The execution of an instruction will require several clock periods. No two microprocessors will use the same number of pulses for their instructions. For this reason, the clock rate of different microprocessors is a misleading measure of performance. Of course, comparing two different clock rates of the same microprocessor, such as comparing a 2MHz to a 4MHz Z80, is indeed relevant. However, this may not even mean that the 4 MHz Z80 will execute 50% faster than the 2MHz Z80, because data and instructions must be fetched from the memory. This implies that all memory access must also be 50% faster, which sometimes is not the case (memory speed must match processor speed).

Let us now look at the *memory performance*. Memory performance is usually characterized by the access time of its RAM, i.e., the time the system takes to fetch a word from the RAM. The faster the RAM, the more expensive the system. Because RAM memory technology progresses constantly, it is difficult to specify a typical speed for a RAM today, as it is virtually assured that there will be a faster one within a year for the same price or lower. Provided the RAM is fast enough, so that an instruction or data may be sent to the microprocessor with no delay, there is no advantage to be gained by using a faster memory. When evaluating the performance of the system, one has to assume that the speed of the RAM is simply sufficient for the speed of the microprocessor. Interestingly enough, some lower-cost systems use slow memory, which slows down the execution of a fast processor. We will assume that most systems being considered have a memory with a speed sufficient for the microprocessor being considered. In that case, the so-called performance of the memory is irrelevant to the choice. We have just lost one of our criteria for selection. Now, how are we going to evaluate the hardware performance?

Benchmarks

The only true way to evaluate the performance of a hardware CPU is to run *benchmark programs.* Benchmark programs are programs that qualify as being "typical of the application considered." A benchmark must be run on several computers and then the timing is compared.

There is no such thing as a "typical instruction" for a computer, and, for this reason, the comparison of specific instructions can be completely misleading. The unfortunate problem is that there is no standard benchmark program. For specific applications, such as a parallel data transfer, a special program can be written, and benchmarks established.

In most cases, the range of applications that must be performed is so wide that it is very difficult to write a reasonable benchmark. A benchmark program written by a manufacturer is almost useless. The manufacturer can only introduce clever improvements, which would make their benchmark program execute more rapidly on their processor than it does on that of the competitor's. To be valid, a benchmark program must be written by the user of the system, since the user is the one who will program the system. However, outside of some specific application programs, there is no such thing as an "average program." Some programs compute heavily, while others perform input-output. There are, therefore, no "standard benchmarks."

If a "general purpose" system is being evaluated, benchmark programs can simply be used as a rough evaluation criterion of the system's performance.

The Important Criteria

The following are important criteria to remember when evaluating a system. First, the actual hardware speed of the MPU is not the most significant selection criterion for overall system performance. Second, most microprocessors on the market today have virtually the same performance. We can argue that the fastest ones are often twice as fast as their leading competitors. However, this will be significant only if the system's software is efficient. The single most important criterion for the operation of a system, if it is to be programmed in a high-level language, is the efficiency of the software. Even if the system is to be programmed in assembly-level language, the skill of the programmer may have a more significant impact on the overall speed of the system than the actual performance of the hardware. In addition, it is likely that within one or two years, faster chips will be available so that speed improvements can be gained at minimal cost by replacing one or more boards. As usual, the speed of the software is the key to system performance.

Finally, the speed bottleneck of a microcomputer system used for personal and business applications is not at the processing level, but at the input-output level. A microcomputer needs a fast disk and printer, both of which are more expensive than the complete microcomputer box. Peripherals usually represent the limiting performance factor for file-oriented processing (business applications).

Most personal and business applications are written in a high-level language, such as BASIC. When using a high-level language, the efficiency of an interpreter (or compiler) is crucial. As an example, some of the poorest BASIC interpreters are 50 times slower than the best. When comparing microprocessors themselves, the ratio of 1 to 2 is usual. When comparing software, a ratio of 1 to 50 or more is not unusual.

How can a user find the best software? Unfortunately, the answer to this question fluctuates rapidly. At the time of this writing, a number of manufacturers have interpreters that are obviously better than others. However, interpreters are continually being improved, so the situation may change rapidly. Any classification here would be misleading. Hobbyist journals (listed at the end of this book) regularly publish comparisons among various interpreters and other programs, by using benchmarks. The interested reader is referred to these measurements.

In summary, the user who is looking for performance in a system is strongly cautioned to check the speed of the software tools he/she will be using.

Complete Hardware

A basic system consists of:
— A microcomputer box, with memory-expansion capability and slots for additional peripheral interfaces, with a sufficient power supply for the reliable operation of a full box.
— An input keyboard of adequate layout.
— A CRT output.
— A hard-copy output (printer).
— A mass memory cassette at a minimum, preferrably a disk.

If the system uses the industry standard S-100 bus, then the completeness of hardware does not matter, as all elements are interchangeable among manufacturers.

However, if the system does not use the S-100 bus, the complete availability of all elements is crucial, especially if future expansion is desired. (S-100 and other buses will be examined in the next section.) The cautious computer buyer should always assume that no additional peripherals or options other than those currently existing will ever be available. A system being demonstrated at a show may be "one of a kind."

Finally, special needs may arise that require a floating-point board or a specific device interface.

The characteristics of all the peripherals used in a system will be presented and evaluated in detail in the next chapter.

Complete Software

A system, however beautiful, is nearly useless unless it is equipped with all of the software facilities required by your application. It must include a monitor, an editor, and a language processor, such as a BASIC interpreter (see Chapter 6 for more details).

Software is very expensive to develop, and many manufacturers try to provide the minimum that they can get away with. In the case of business applications, the following criteria may be applied:

1. Availability of ready-to-use business packages ready to run on your system, whatever the language.
2. A complete BASIC (see Chapter 7 for details).
3. A good file system, for automatic management of your files.

For an educational system:

1. Availability of a complete BASIC.
2. Availability of time-sharing software for multiple access to the system by several users simultaneously.

For a personal system:

1. A complete BASIC.
2. A good file system.
3. An assembler (if desired).

Note: this latter point might seem obvious. However, as of this writing, some "personal computers" are equipped with an acceptable BASIC, but not with an acceptable assembler, nor any linkage between both, thus, precluding the convenient use of assembly language routines.

In addition, and in all cases, there should be a complete and powerful editor for convenient editing.

Convenience

Convenience is one of the keys to successful system utilization. Most users do not care to reinvent the wheel. Sometimes, however, it is necessary to either create complex interfaces, or reprogram algorithms that were invented long ago. For this reason, the most popular microprocessors in previous applications have usually become the most popular in personal microcomputers. Most microcomputers use the Intel 8080, the Zilog Z80, the Motorola 6800, or the MOS Technology 6502. Interestingly, Zilog is an offshoot of Intel, while MOS Technology is an offshoot of Motorola. Because of the wealth of software available for the 8080 or the Z80 (they have a common instruction set), as well as for the Motorola 6800 and, to a smaller extent, for the MOS Technology 6502, these microprocessors are now the most widely used as personal microcomputers.

Convenience means that all of the functions required to put the system into immediate use are available, and that the time and effort required to do this are minimal.

To be more specific, convenience means:

1. A complete system is ready to use from both a hardware and software standpoint.
2. Ease of operation. This includes mostly powerful software aids (editor, interpreter, file system), and easy-to-use hardware (fast disk, fast printer).
3. Immediate availability and applicability.
4. Excellent documentation, which is often a key factor for the efficient use of your time.

Performance of the Overall System

If the computer system is used to manipulate files, rather than execute programs (which process data that is resident within the central memory of the system), the efficiency of the mass storage device is essential to the performance of the system. Particularly for business applications, the files will be large, and cannot reside simultaneously in the central memory of the system (limited to 48K or 64K, of which 3K to 10K is usually used up by the ROM monitor program). The speed of the disk, whether a floppy disk or a hard disk, becomes crucial. In fact, the access time of the disk is more important than the execution speed of the processor in cases where repeated access to files is needed (e.g., business applications).

If a large number of files needs to be printed, a high-speed printer will become necessary, otherwise the operation of the system will be significantly slowed down. A high-speed printer is usually the most expensive peripheral. For this reason, low-cost printers are often used instead of high-speed ones, resulting in overall system inefficiency, as the user must wait for the file to be completely printed before he/she can continue work.

Reliability

When first designed, most microcomputer systems were not built to the same reliability standards as older minicomputers. They were built with enthusiasm by a single engineer, and found a market by accident. They could then no longer be improved, as their configuration had in fact been standardized because of the very number of sales. The cost of changing the design or the documentation was prohibitive for small companies. In addition, the large demand for these early microcomputers led some suppliers to use lower-cost, unreliable components. As a result, many of the early buyers did experience reliability problems.

However, this is no longer the case. The LSI circuits integrate so many transistors in a single chip that a complete computer uses far fewer circuits than in the past. This reduction in the parts count has resulted in highly increased reliability, compared with traditional computer designs. Contemporary microcomputers are very reliable. They will be even more reliable in the future. Most users simply never experience a failure.

For all practical purposes, microcomputers are highly reliable in a "normal" environment after they have worked correctly for the first 200 hours. This test-period is called the "burn-in" phase; most malfunctions will occur during this time. The probability of failures happening after this period is much smaller. A "normal" environment means that there are no extreme variations of temperature or humidity.

The primary danger stems from the enormous success of micro-computer systems. In order to continue providing systems at an even lower cost, some manufacturers occasionally turn to less reliable part suppliers. It is possible to purchase parts that have not been tested at a much lower cost (in the "grey" market). This would work fine, provided that the parts are tested on arrival. However, because of time pressures, this may not always happen, so that untested and potentially unreliable parts may occasionally be included within a system.

The unfortunate fact is that the failure resulting from inferior parts might occur during a relatively infrequent event, such as at low temperature, high temperature or simply through progressive deterioration of the component. And, this might happen after the guarantee has expired. Usually, the manufacturer will still replace the faulty component. However, tracing the failure down to the faulty component can be a time-consuming and frustrating task. The reliability of the manufacturer and his/her reputation are therefore a significant criterion for selection.

TYPES OF SYSTEMS

Kit, Board or System?

Microcomputers come in two main shapes: single-board microcomputers, and complete systems packaged in attractive boxes. Microcomputers are also available as a completely assembled system or as a kit.

Each type of system has advantages and limitations. A board has the advantage of minimum cost, and the disadvantage of limited hardware resources. A box offers the hardware capabilities of a traditional minicomputer, but costs more. Let us now examine the alternatives in detail.

Single-Board Microcomputer

A typical board includes: the microprocessor unit plus any required control chips, a limited amount of memory (such as 512 words of ROM, and 2K to 4K of RAM), and a minimum number of interfaces (such as a teletype interface, a tape cassette interface, and general-purpose input-output ports).

Because of its standardized structure, a board can easily be manufactured in large quantities at a low cost. However, because of the limited board area available, the buyer must compromise between the various facilities that might reside on the board. These options include the quantity of memory, I/O ports and interfaces, and the presence of a keyboard. We will show that memory limitation is usually the most serious, as it precludes the use of an assembler or of a high-level language.

In view of these limitations, a board can be used by itself for essentially two purposes:

1. As a control device. Such a board provides the processing power of a complete microcomputer at a cost of $100 to $500. It can be used to advantage to directly control relays, motors, or other devices. It is an inexpensive, programmable, general-purpose, control device which can be used in a number of ways. Its main application is in industrial automation, but it is also possible, in a home or office environment to use it to control simple applications such as motor regulation, process control, environment monitoring, burglar alarms, automatic timing of lights or water sprinklers.

2. As an educational tool. A board has significant value for understanding the interconnect of a typical microcomputer system, as well as for learning to program in machine language. In this role, it is, however, essentially a toy. It is not reasonably possible to develop long or complex programs on a single board. Because of the limited amount of memory included on the board, it is usually not capable of running *assembler* or *interpreter* programs. For that reason, it is necessary, on most boards, to enter instructions through the keyboard as a sequence of hexadecimal numbers. This process is lengthy and prone to errors. Most users will be able to enter perhaps a few dozen instructions in this way, and thus learn all of the basics of programming at the machine level. If a sufficient amount of memory is included (usually as an external board), it may be possible to execute an assembler program on the board. This allows the use of *symbolic* programs. However, writing symbolic programs requires the availability of an *alphanumeric keyboard,* or a standard input-output device such as a Teletype. If $1,000 to $1,500 are going to be spent on a Teletype, we might reasonably argue that this is a better choice than a single board.

To summarize, a board is a very inexpensive computing device that can be used efficiently as a dedicated controller, or as a limited educational tool for understanding the structure of a microcomputer and learning elementary programming. As a final example, a single board may be used inside a business machine, but not as a business system.

The Microcomputer System

The microcomputer itself consists of one or more boards packaged in an attractive box and supplemented by a minimal quantity of peripherals required to make reasonable use of the system. Complete

Getting the right board may be difficult.

systems are now available for as little as $500, or just about twice the cost of a single board. For this reason, they offer a much more desirable alternative for personal use. A typical *system* includes the computer box plus an *alphanumeric keyboard,* a *CRT display,* and a *mass memory device.* The most inexpensive systems provide a *tape cassette* mass memory, while the more powerful ones provide *floppy disk drives.* In addition, for any practical application, a *printer* is required.

In theory, a microcomputer system can do anything a computer system can do, within its hardware and software limitations. Its essential disadvantage is to be less powerful than a traditional minicomputer, i.e., slower and with more restricted memory and input-output capabilities. Two types of systems can be differentiated: minimal cost systems and general-purpose microcomputers.

The Minimal Cost System

Minimal cost systems include the microcomputer box with 4K words of memory, the enclosure, the power supply, the keyboard, a CRT monitor, and a tape cassette.

This configuration has the same raw processing power as any other microcomputer, but is limited by its memory and peripherals. The memory can usually be expanded, and alternative peripherals are often available. However, "continuous software" is usually not available. The *operating system* program required to support the various peripherals and sizes of memory must be designed correctly from the start. A minimal system is designed as just that. It includes a minimal operating system called the *monitor,* which manages the keyboard and the cassette. The switchover to a larger configuration requires a different operating system.

The minimal cost system offers an assembler program, and a mini-BASIC, or other interpreter program. The user may now write symbolic, assembly-level programs, or programs in (simplified) BASIC. In addition, the user may store or retrieve these programs on tape cassettes, an important convenience. Such a system normally comes with tape cassettes containing a variety of programs such as games or "useful" programs; e.g., checkbook management, arithmetic education, etc. Again, this system is limited by its memory and peripherals. It can be used for personal purposes, but not as a business system.

This example illustrates a fact which has been central to all computer systems: the cost of the processing unit itself is a small fraction of the total cost of a useful system. The dominant hardware cost is, and always has been, the cost of the peripherals.

The microcomputer board need not be housed in a large box. It is often contained in the keyboard or in the CRT enclosure.

In summary, minimal cost systems are enjoyable educational toys with which it is possible to play games, run a number of educational programs, or learn programming. However, because they are equipped with a small amount of memory and a slow mass storage device (the cassette), they are not usable as business systems, as they cannot provide efficient file management. They can indeed be used for a large number of personal applications. Provided that additional memory is purchased, they can run an assembler, an editor, or an interpreter program, and thus support most applications. However, it must be noted that some of these systems offer the capability to upgrade to a general-purpose microcomputer system. This is an important consideration when selecting a system.

The General-Purpose Microcomputer

The general-purpose microcomputer is the functional equivalent of what the minicomputer used to be. It is a box containing a processor board plus additional boards required for memory and input-output interfacing. The box is partially empty, allowing the insertion of additional boards so that memory can be expanded to 48K or 64K. Several additional boards can then be inserted for connecting to a number of additional input-output devices. A typical system comes equipped with peripherals: one or preferably two floppy disk drives, a good quality alphanumeric keyboard, and a good quality CRT display. In addition, a suitable printer must be added to the system. A general-purpose microcomputer should also include a power supply capable of driving the maximum number of boards with which the microcomputer may be equipped. Such a system is no longer limited by the previous shortcomings, and is essentially capable of running any kind of program that does not tax its processing capabilities.

Practically, the microcomputer may be packaged in the keyboard box, the CRT box, or in a variety of boxes. For flexibility in adding additional boards, it is usually packaged in a separate box the size of a hi-fi tuner.

The advantages of a microcomputer over a traditional minicomputer are:

— Lower cost (perhaps ten times less).
— Smaller size.
— Lower power consumption and power dissipation, resulting in a smaller and cheaper power supply and the need for fewer ventilation fans. This also allows the possibility of elegant packaging, in a style close to home hi-fi equipment.
— Availability of new low cost peripherals.

The main limitations of a microcomputer as compared to a minicomputer are:

— Less processing power. The use of an 8-bit microprocessor results in a slower execution speed. However, this limitation is generally not felt, except in the case of arithmetic computations. The low cost of the microcomputer allows it to be used for a dedicated task, eliminating the need for complex task management or time-sharing software. The processing power of a microcomputer is sufficient for most personal and business applications.
— Less software. Because microprocessors have been developed more recently, their software library is smaller than that of traditional minicomputers. However, the gap is being reduced constantly, and a large amount of software will soon be available.
— Less I/O capability. A microcomputer has a limited input-output bandwidth as compared to a mini. Again, however, this has little practical impact for most uses.

In summary, a microcomputer offers most of the characteristics of former minicomputers, except that the numeric processing of a microcomputer is slower, at a fraction of their cost. Microcomputers will not eliminate minicomputers; they have simply created a new market, where it is possible to dedicate a microcomputer to a specific task. For all practical purposes, however, the microcomputer simply brings the data processing power of a "mini" to any user.

Front Panel or No Front Panel?

Some microcomputer boxes come equipped with a front panel, others are supplied without it. A front panel is simply a row of lights and a row of switches, plus miscellaneous lights, switches or buttons. A front panel is designed to facilitate hands-on debugging when programming in assembly language. It displays the binary contents of the buses and the registers in a visible form. For control applications, which will usually be programmed in assembly-level language, the presence of a front panel is favored by most programmers who have an understanding of hardware, as it instantly visualizes the condition of registers or buses. With a front panel, there is no need to submit a sequence of orders in order to obtain this information. However, the cost of the front panel is high, as it requires a separate controller board plus a special program within the system. It adds perhaps $100 to the cost. For this reason, most microcomputer systems today come without a front panel. If the intent is to use the system primarily in a high-level language, the front panel is simply useless. Even if the user intends to program the system in assembly-level language, the non-availability of a front panel may not be a significant disadvantage. The user who has never known a front panel will never know what he/she is missing, since all debugging facilities can be obtained at the terminal.

Front panels were provided on early microcomputers (Altair, Imsai), as they were expected to be used in a traditional laboratory environment. Generally, however, front panels are no longer provided. On a business machine, they are simply unnecessary. If the user programs in BASIC, the front panel will never be used.

The absence of a front panel does not make it impossible to check the contents of internal registers. The task simply becomes more cumbersome, and is done from the console (CRT or Teletype).

Finally, a system with no front panel just needs an ON-OFF key or switch; it looks nicer, is simpler to use, and has, therefore, more appeal. For these reasons, the majority of microcomputers now no longer have a front panel.

Which Bus?

Most microcomputers today provide an internal connection through a standardized "bus." This bus has 50 to 100 lines, and carries the necessary signals between the boards of the system. The most popular one is the S-100 bus originally introduced by Altair and then used by Imsai and many others. It is based on the 8080, and can be used with a Z80. It cannot be used by a 6800 in any reasonable way. A number of other buses exist, such as the SS50 (for the 6800) and the IEEE-488. Generally speaking, if simplicity and convenience in connecting additional devices are required, the S-100 bus has a definite advantage, because it is by far the most widely available. Most common boards are now available with an interface for an S-100, and sometimes for other buses. Even though the choice may be somewhat more restricted for a bus other than S-100, this is not a significant constraint in view of the wide choice available.

In short, if maximum flexibility in the choice of a peripheral is felt to be a strong advantage, S-100 would qualify. Generally, however, a standardized bus need not have a major impact on system selection if a complete system is available from the manufacturer.

The Connectors in the Back

At least three connectors are desirable:
1. The Teletype 20mA current loop. This is a classic serial port for a TTY, or other slow terminal. Various 4-wire connectors are used.
2. The standard RS-232C interface. The connector is indispensable. It may be used with any device equipped with an EIA (RS-232C) interface and will almost always be used for the CRT. Several terminals may be connected to the same port in parallel.
3. A parallel printer interface. Specialized 8-bit parallel output for a fast printer.

Caution: most microprocessors have a single *serial* I/O port. In the latter case, both the RS-232C connector, and the 20mA current loop socket are connected to it in parallel.

This means that two devices, such as a CRT and a Teletype, may each be connected to one socket simultaneously, but normally may not be used simultantously. On input, both keyboards should clearly not be used at the same time.

On output, they may remain connected at the same time if both operate at the same speed (110 baud, or 10 characters per second, for a TTY). However, a CRT is normally set to a much higher baud rate (up to 9600 baud).

The availability of both the RS-232C and the 20mA connectors is a convenience. It does not mean that two terminals may be connected and operated simultaneously (this would require two serial ports).

On the other hand, and provided that the microprocessor is equipped with a parallel port, a high-speed parallel printer may operate simultaneously.

Kit or Assembled?

A kit typically offers significant savings to the potential buyer when compared to assembled systems. If the intent is to save money, a kit may be purchased and the educational value of assembling the system, as well as the psychological satisfaction, are probably worth the try. However, in the case of a microcomputer box, we should stress that the quality of actual assembly is important to the reliable operation of the system being built. For this reason, an inexperienced user might be better off buying an assembled system, and spending his/her time learning how to program the system usefully rather than spending long nights trying to isolate faulty connections or components. The savings offered by assembling a kit are not likely to be realized if the user does not have adequate testing equipment available. Adequate testing tools can be very expensive, and can completely wipe out any financial advantage gained from the assembly labor. The unavailability of such tools might lead to errors in the operation of the system, which will only show up later, when unusual combinations are met, and ruin the value of the system or its reliability.

Another problem has come up recently: unreliable components. Several manufacturer rejects of kits have disappeared from leading semiconductor manufacturers, been relabeled, and have appeared on the consumer market.

Little can be done about this. The problem with a kit is that, if it does not work, then the user must isolate the faulty component. With an assembled system, the situation is somewhat better. However, faulty components may fail only after a year or so, or at high temperature.

To the credit of microcomputers, we must note that:
— They are intrinsically more reliable than traditional minicomputers, because they have fewer parts.
— They are easy to fix, and the cost of replacing an entire board is small.

In summary, be wary, but do not be afraid. We suggest that you learn programming rather than soldering. However, the savings realized by purchasing a kit might make a system accessible to you where it would not be otherwise.

SUMMARY

This chapter discussed the criteria that are important when selecting the right system for your needs.

Software support is probably the key to system selection. If a system is intended to be used in a wide variety of applications, most users do not care to reprogram the system every time. They would prefer the immediate availability of software (packages that they can plug into the system and use for their specific applications). The availability of a large library of programs, conveniently usable on a system, is probably one of the first keys to successful system selection. In addition, the system should offer the required hardware facilities and ease in adding new devices that may be required for the specific application intended by the user.

9

THE PERIPHERALS

INTRODUCTION

The selection of suitable peripherals may be more complex than that of the "mainframe," i.e., the microcomputer proper. The peripherals selected also generally have the largest impact on the cost and usability of the system.

In this chapter, all of the usual peripherals will be examined and evaluated: first, input devices (the keyboard), then, output devices (display, printer), mass memory devices (disks, tapes), and finally, special devices (voice input-output, light pen, etc.).

THE KEYBOARD

Often, the keyboard is incorporated either in the mainframe assembly, or the CRT display unit. Most keyboards, however, are separate units.

Fortunately, relatively few options exist for the choice of a keyboard. Common sense should be used in selecting one. A keyboard must be sturdy, reliable, and offer good contacts. The layout must be practical for the application considered. A feature to look for is *multiple key rollover* protection. A problem occurs when several keys are depressed simultaneously, or almost simultaneously. This can occur, for example, during rapid data entry. Simple keyboards may ignore, refuse or discard the additional keys pressed. A "protected" keyboard will automatically store multiple-key closures, as long as they are not simultaneous.

For the business user: a simple alphanumeric keyboard is not sufficient. A full "business keyboard" is required, with the usual alphanumeric keys, a separate numeric keyboard with the 10 digits, the cursor control for the screen (up, down, left, right), plus control keys (reset, etc.).

OUTPUT DEVICES

The CRT Display

The CRT display has become the universal output medium for micro-computer systems. This is because it is silent, and will display a large amount of text in a small amount of time, by moving it vertically (called *scrolling.*) In addition, a CRT *monitor* that can be easily integrated into a design can be purchased for less than $100.

Three types of displays may be distinguished:
1. The traditional TV set
2. The simple monitor
3. The video display terminal (VDT).

These three possibilities will now be examined.

The Video Display Terminal

The VDT or CRT terminal is a terminal built with a monitor, a key-board, and control electronics (for cursor control, keyboard control, screen functions, and local memory). It has been the traditional terminal for communicating with computer systems, and is one of those best-suited to a business environment because of its professional design

Figure 9-1:   Lear Siegler "Dumb Terminal" is a basic CRT terminal. It features a 12-inch screen, 59 keys, 24 rows of 80 letters, RS-232 and 20mA connectors (64 ASCII characters, 5 × 7 dot matrix).

Figure 9-2:   Typical QWERTY Keyboard and decoding electronics

and convenience features. However, it is the most expensive alternative ($700 and up, depending upon features).

A combination of keyboard, video monitor, and software can provide equivalent services.

The Video Monitor

A video monitor is simply a TV set without the tuning, separation and amplification electronics (i.e., the speaker, channel selectors, etc.) As it does not need to detect UHF/VHF frequencies, a monitor has a direct video entry connection, and can accommodate signals of much higher bandwidth than in the case of a regular TV. In particular, 80 character lines are possible.

Every TV includes a monitor, and can be modified for direct video entry.

The Conventional TV Set

Inasmuch as it may be available "free," the conventional TV set may be the most inexpensive display. However, if one connects directly to the antenna (as in TV games), the resulting bandwidth limitation results in short character lines on the screen.

However, in the case of color displays, alternatives are so expensive as to make the TV a preferential choice. Remember that the short-line limitation remains.

In view of the very low cost of a black and white monitor (and its

Figure 9-3: Soroc IQ 120 is another basic CRT terminal featuring 24 rows of 80 characters, numeric pad, upper and lower case.

higher bandwidth), there is virtually no advantage to purchasing a black and white TV.

Displaying Text on a Screen

Let us now examine the features common to all displays. The purpose of any screen is to display text, and, if possible, to allow some graphics.

Images are displayed on a traditional television set by illuminating tiny dots on the screen. To display characters, the dots are much larger in order to be "clearly visible." Each character is defined by a *dot matrix* (see Figure 9-4). Each character is displayed by illuminating dots in a rectangle, each rectangle having, for example, 7 rows of 5 dots each. For better definition, more dots are used, for example, a 7 × 9 dot matrix. However, this reduces the maximum number of characters of a given size that may be displayed on the screen. The 5 × 7 matrix is used on low cost systems. However, it is difficult to distinguish lower case from upper case, and to extend lower case letters below the line with so few dots.

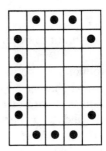 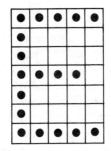 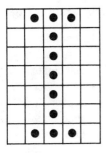

Figure 9-4:   A 5 × 7 dot matrix

The following is an interesting technical question. We have shown that a CRT receives characters from the computer as bytes, i.e., groups of 8 bits (each character corresponds to a unique 8-bit combination in the ASCII code). Therefore, how are these 8 bits converted to 35 or more dots on the screen? The answer is: by using memory (ROM) chips. For each 8-bit code, a group of memory locations will supply the dot pattern. However, there are a few consequences. Because it is easy to replace ROM chips, it is a simple task to modify a character set. Professional displays may offer alternate character sets, ranging from APL to foreign languages.

The Lines and Characters

Clearly, the user would like as many characters, and as many lines, as possible. In the case of a television set, where the computer connects to the antenna, the limited bandwidth of a set restricts the user to about 24 lines of 40 characters, if he/she uses a good quality set, a 5 × 7 matrix, and only upper case characters. A 24 character width is common.

In the case of a monitor, or a VDT, the computer connects directly to the video input, significantly improving the bandwidth. 24 lines of 80 characters (upper and lower case) are almost standard.

For the business user: the standard line length for business purposes is 80 characters (the width of an IBM card); ideally, it should be 120 or 132. A TV set is not acceptable, unless modified for direct video-connection, in which case it is used as a monitor. For business purposes, the minimum line length is also considered to be 24 lines.

Standard printers print 80 characters per line or even more (132), hence the obvious advantage of an 80 character line.

Additional CRT Features

Most additional features are implemented by a program, or sometimes by a more complex controller board. They include:

— The cursor: every CRT must display a cursor to indicate a position on the screen, usually the position where the next character will appear. The appearance of a cursor is typically a square or an underline. Its appearance may be programmable, and it may blink.
— The system may offer two shades, grey and white (useful to separate questions from answers) or even reverse (black on white).
— Characters or cursor may be made to blink.
— Limited graphics may be available. Typically, they are implemented by selecting specific dots of the dot matrix used to display characters.
— Color is an obvious option. If a color set is used, four "colors" are commonly available: black, white, violet, green.

Dumb versus Intelligent

Additional features may be obtained by transferring to the display terminal some of the functions performed by the microcomputer. Instead of a "dumb terminal," it becomes an "intelligent terminal."

An intelligent terminal is usually designed to be useful "off line," i.e., disconnected from the computer. It offers local memory (for data storage), and editing functions (for correcting errors). In view of the low cost of microcomputers, intelligent CRT terminals tend not to be used in this new environment.

Display Summary

For the personal user: for color displays, the only low cost option is the home TV set. For black and white displays, a commercial TV will limit you to 16 lines of 32 characters (approximately). A *monitor* is recommended.

For the business user: when the microcomputer box does not include a keyboard, a *terminal* is needed. A "dumb" one is normally sufficient. You will get 24 lines of 80 characters, upper and lower case. Watch for a full keyboard on the terminal. A 12-inch screen is considered optimal. A 7 × 9 dot matrix or better is required for easy reading.

If the microcomputer box includes the required keyboard, you may simply add a 12-inch monitor, plus the required CRT controller board in the microcomputer (if available), and obtain equivalent functions.

Talking to the Display

Several input devices have been invented to point to specific locations on a keyboard. The most frequently used ones will be described at the end of this chapter. They are: the light pen, the joystick, and to a smaller extent, the "Mouse."

The Printer

A CRT display provides "soft copy." The user can move information quickly across the screen ("scrolling"), and even "flip pages" ("paging"). In a business environment, using a printer to obtain "hard copy" (on paper) is usually desirable.

Why not just use the office Selectric? Suitably modified, the office Selectric can be used. However, it is expensive, relatively slow (30 characters per second or "cps"), and may not be sufficiently reliable unless designed as a computer terminal. This option will be reviewed below.

You might ask: why not photograph the CRT display? This would not be practical, in view of the very small photos. However, it is technically feasible to couple a display to an office copier. This might become an alternative in the future.

Let us now consider the range of alternatives. Naturally, we want:
— Low cost
— High printing quality
— Speed
— Reliability
— Low noise

The final choice, as usual, will be a compromise. Four main types of printers may be distinguished:
— Thermal/Electrosensitive
— Band printer
— Matrix printer
— Line printer

They will now be examined in view of the goals just stated.

Thermal and Electrosensitive Printer

Thermal printers use a special paper and burn characters into it. The printing element has dots or segments that press on the paper, and the proper combination of segments is energized to burn the required character.

Because the printing element is simple, and has no moving parts, these printers are inexpensive and silent. However, they offer a mediocre printing quality (compared to a good Selectric), cannot operate at high speed (because of the time it takes to burn characters), and require special paper.

Electrosensitive and other thermal printers are usually utilized for the lowest cost printers aimed at minimal capability (short line width, low speed). However, there are notable exceptions, such as the Texas Instruments Silent Terminal, which may be used for up to 99 cps.

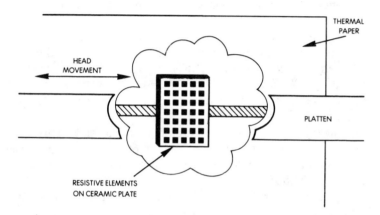

Figure 9-5:   A dot-matrix thermal printer

Band Printer

Impact printers are most frequently used. Their principle of operation is to use a printing head and move it, or else to use multiple heads.

A band printer operates essentially like an office Selectric, by moving the head across the paper. Three main techniques are used for the head:

1. A cylindrical or spherical element with all of the characters
2. A daisy wheel
3. A matrix of needles.

(This latter case will be studied in the next section.)

The Cylinder Head

The cylinder head technique is used by one of the oldest computer terminals, the Teletype (an abbreviation for "teletypewriter"-name trademarked). A cylindrical printing head is used (see Figure 9-6) which has 4 rows of characters, can rotate into 17 positions, and can be raised. In order to print a character, the cylinder is rotated to the appropriate position, raised to the required row level, and then hit with a hammer. The character presses the ribbon against the paper. All linkages are electromechanical and use cams actuated by electromagnets.

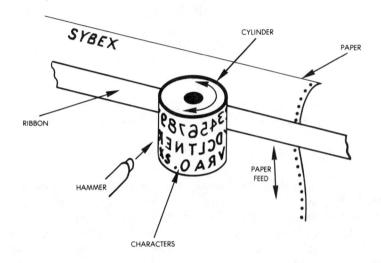

Figure 9-6:   The Teletype printing cylinder

The standard KSR33 Teletype operates at 10 cps. It is noisy and slow but reliable and low in cost (a little over $1000), and has excellent readability. It is also limited to upper case. Within its price range, the Teletype is still a good choice as a slow, readable and reliable printer. It cannot be considered for business applications.

Many other models exist. In particular, the ASR33 is a KSR33 equipped with a paper tape reader punch for a small additional cost. (ASR stands for "Automatic Send Receive," while KSR stands for "Keyboard Send Receive.") In the past, this was valuable as a "hard copy" for programs at a time when floppy disks did not exist, and can still be used in small systems, if available. In practice, it is now obsolete in a disk-based system.

The two standard Teletype interfaces are RS-232C and the 20mA current loop. The Teletype uses ASCII code.

Figure 9-7:   The traditional Teletype

The Selectric

The Selectric is IBM's converted typewriter, which uses a sphere of metallized plastic that can tilt and rotate. It is also slow (15 cps to 30 cps), but offers a printing quality identical to an office typewriter. The Selectric's cost is somewhat higher than that of the Teletype, but it may be used in a minimal business application. It has upper and lower case and changeable printing elements, but is still unsuitable for continuous operation or long lists.

The Daisy Wheel Printer

The daisy wheel printer uses a wheel with up to 100 characters (see Figure 9-8). Each character is on an individual arm, so that only a rotation is needed. The hammer hits only a single letter. It is possible to guarantee accurate positioning and uniform striking; this allows fast, quiet, and reliable operation, with superb print quality.

The picture of an actual daisy wheel appears in Figure 9-8. Wheels are changeable, so that various character sets can be used, and are standard for several manufacturers (Diablo, Qume).

The printing quality is so high that text justification is often provided, resulting in camera ready copy.

For the business user: the daisy wheel printer is the current optimal printer for a microcomputer system, but costs $3000 to $5000, which probably makes it the most expensive component of a system.

Figure 9-8:   A daisy wheel shows individual characters

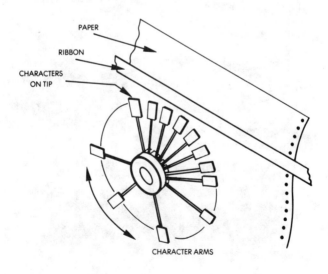

Figure 9-9:   The daisy wheel rotates in a circle

Figure 9-10:   Diablo Hyterm is a daisy wheel printer with 94 characters, 45 cps.

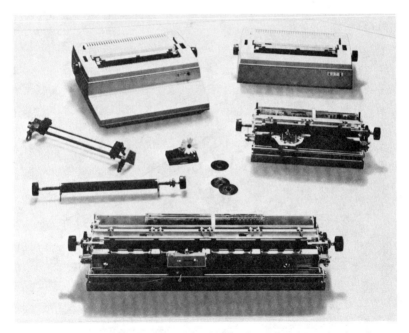

Figure 9-11:   Qume Sprint Micro 3 Family offers lower cost daisy wheel quality

Matrix Printer

A matrix printer uses pins to print a pattern of dots on paper. The characters are generated just as in the case of the CRT display, by selecting the appropriate combinations of pins in a rectangle of 5 rows by 7 columns or 7 rows by 9 columns. Each pin is equipped with a coil. When energized, the pin is thrown against the ribbon, printing a dot on the paper. For each character, seven or nine lines of dots are printed. However, the inertia is minimal, so that fast operation is possible.

In a low cost system, a single head is used, which prints character by character, and moves across the paper. In a higher cost system, an entire line of needles is available for 80 or 120 characters. A whole line is printed in just seven or nine steps. This is illustrated in Figure 9-13.

The general advantages of a matrix printer are: relatively low cost, high speed, and quiet operation. The main disadvantage is the relatively poor quality of printing. The printing quality is sufficient for the eye, but not for reproduction or business letters.

A well-known matrix printer is the Decwriter, which offers 30 cps operation, and unusually high quality.

For the business user: the matrix printer is a good alternative to the daisy wheel printer at almost half the cost, as long as no business letters need to be generated.

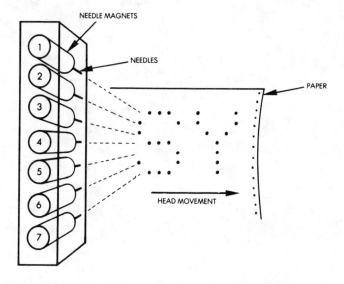

Figure 9-12:   Seven needles may hit paper simultaneously

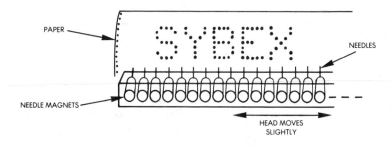

Figure 9-13: A whole line of dots is printed at once

The Chain Printer

One kind of printer has not even been mentioned here: the chain printer. Chain printers can attain a speed of more than 1,000 lines per minute. They are used for large computers, and sometimes for mini-computers. However, their cost is simply so high that it would not make sense to connect them to a low cost microcomputer. If the user invests in the very high cost of a high speed chain printer, he/she might as well invest in a large, powerful computer to drive it.

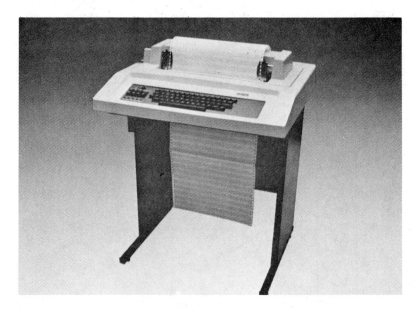

Figure 9-14: The LA-36 Decwriter is a high quality 30 cps matrix printer. It uses a 7 × 7 dot matrix and has the full 128 character set.

The chain printer shown in Figure 9-15 is a drum type. The character is moved around the drum to the required printing position.

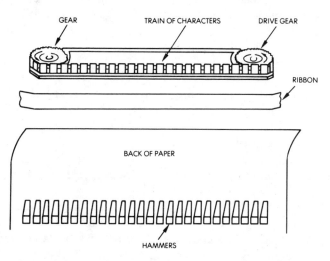

Figure 9-15:   A drum type printer

The Line Printer

In contrast to 200 to 300 lines per minute maximum for the previous printers, a line printer will operate up to 2000 lpm. It will not be described here as its price is simply out of proportion to a micro-computer system.

Superprinters

In the largest computer installations, where cost is no longer a consideration, non-impact printers are used for super-speed. An *ink jet* printer operates by projecting small ink droplets and deflecting them electrostatically. Speeds of 40,000 lines per minute may be achieved.

In the *laser writer,* the paper is charged electrostatically, and attracts dry ink powder (as in a photo-copying machine). The pattern is then baked into the paper. Many lines are printed simultaneously, and speeds of 20,000 lines per minute are achieved.

Printers for Business: A Summary

Three essential alternatives have been indicated. The best choices are the daisy wheel printer for high quality, and the line printer for speed; the printer then becomes the most expensive part of a system.

Note that one essential "option," a sprocket feed, is needed if any business forms, labels, or checks are to be printed. No friction mechanism can provide the required vertical accuracy to position forms correctly.

DISKS

Because the main memory inside the microcomputer box is usually limited to about 64K bytes, and is volatile, large programs and files must be stored on a permanent medium. Either disks or tapes are used. The relative merits of each will be presented. We will show that the "minifloppy" has become a preferred solution for hobbyists, while the standard floppy or the Winchester disk are preferred for business applications.

A disk is coated on one or both sides with a magnetic oxide that rotates permanently. A read/write head, much like the head of a tape recorder, is positioned over a "track" of the disk. Data can then be "written" on the disk as a sequence of bits. The "0's" and "1's" are written on the surface of the track by magnetizing particles in one direction or another. Information stored in this manner is "permanent," as long as no strong magnetic field is applied to the disk.

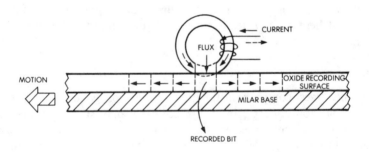

Figure 9-16:   Recording a bit on a disk

The concentric tracks on the disk appear in Figure 9-17.

In order to be able to retrieve information from the disk, the user needs to know on which track it is stored, and where.

To retrieve information conveniently within a track, the standard practice has been to divide each track into sectors. This is illustrated in

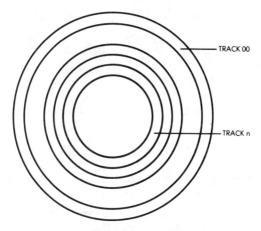

Figure 9-17:   The tracks on the disk

Figure 9-18. A typical sector has 128 bytes. Information will now be retrieved by its sector and track number.

Of course, no one wants to worry about the actual allocation of sectors to a file when using the system. A good DOS (Disk Operating System) program will manage all disk usage and provide an FMS (File Management System) so that we can type:

"LOAD NEW FROM DISK"

and the six sectors used by program "NEW" will be automatically retrieved from the disk. This is called "symbolic file naming."

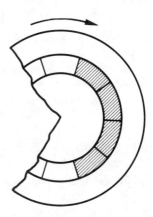

Figure 9-18:   A 4-block sequential file is stored on four sectors

The hard disk has been the traditional media for mass storage. It offers high speed and high capacity. Unfortunately, until recently, it was very costly, and was not used with microcomputers. However, new, smaller "hard disks" have now become available: the Winchester disks. Both floppies and Winchester disks will now be described.

The Floppy Disk

The floppy disk operates just like the hard disk, except that it is smaller and "floppy"; the disk is soft and is permanently contained in a cardboard case. The disk itself rotates inside its case. The inside of the cardboard is coated with a special low-friction material, and has an opening through which the read/write head can make contact with the disk.

Floppy disk formats, unlike hard disks, have been standardized (by IBM), and prices tend to be similar for most manufacturers. The original 8" floppy was introduced by IBM with the 3740 in the late 1960's.

A floppy is a complex mechanical device, and requires a "controller board" that will decode commands from the microcomputer and carry them out, as well as manage data transfers. Normally, it must be added to the microcomputer box.

The Minifloppy

The minifloppy is a smaller version of the floppy: 5.25 inches instead of 8 inches. It was introduced by Shugart in the fall of 1976, and they established the data formats (not IBM). The minifloppy encountered great success in the microcomputer industry because it offers bulk storage at low cost (a diskette itself costs $5-$10). The traditional floppy has 35 to 40 tracks, depending on the head-positioning mechanism. One manufacturer (Micropolis) provides 77 tracks, i.e., twice the amount of storage, and still claims sufficient reliability.

The normal minifloppy provides about one third the storage of the regular floppy. It can be used to great advantage in a hobby environment, and for maintaining personal files and programs.

For the business user: The capacity of a minifloppy is too small. The minimum required is a regular floppy. Even a regular floppy is inconvenient for a large inventory or mailing list.

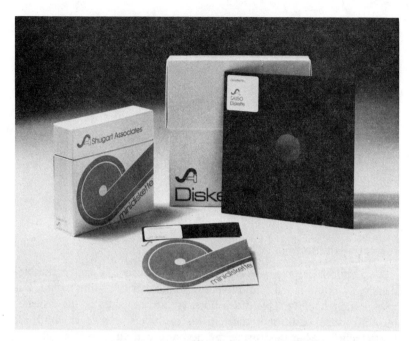

Figure 9-19: Diskette and minidiskette

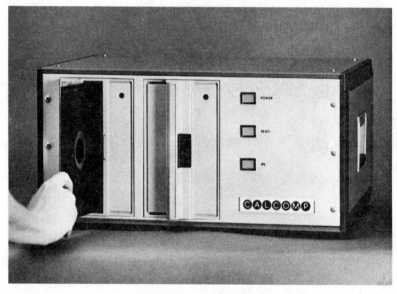

Figure 9-20: Inserting a floppy

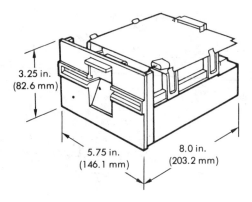

Figure 9-21:   Size of mini-floppy

Increasing the Storage

Two options are available for doubling the storage capacity: double-density and dual-sided. *Double-density* packs twice as much data, but loses some reliability. *Dual-sided* floppies use both sides of the diskette, but introduce additional mechanical problems. However, both of these techniques are maturing rapidly, and can already be used with acceptable reliability.

Figure 9-22:   Persci 277 dual diskette drive manages two diskettes with a size of only 8.6″ × 4.4″ × 15″.

One or Two Disks?

If you plan to copy a program or a file from one disk to another, alphabetize, or merge two diskettes, you need two disks. If you want more (readily available) storage space, then you need two, three or four disks.

Every system should have two disks. Anything less limits the capabilities of the system (but may be acceptable for simple personal computing).

For the business user: at a minimum, two disks are indispensable.

Winchester Disks

Hard disks were introduced by IBM in 1956, and were used on large computers for fast bulk storage. Recently, Winchester head technology was introduced to alleviate the problems encountered in traditional disk designs, and to provide improved density. In this technology, the head loading force is typically only 10 grams. The head has a very low mass, and takes off and lands on the disk surface itself. When the disk is not moving, the head rests on the disk. When the disk is moving, the head flies on a thin layer of air. Winchester disks are designed so that the head will also almost always land and take off in a reserved area on the disk, thereby minimizing the risk to the data stored on it. The head and its carriage are incorporated into the disk pack or the disk unit, eliminating the disk alignment problem. Also, modules are sealed to prevent contamination. The original IBM data module (the 3340) was removable, but the cost per module was large. Recently developed systems are fixed units, and are not removable.

Winchester disk drives are quiet, very reliable, light (5 to 10 kilos), and use very little power (50 to 100 watts for the 8-inch version). Typical capacities are 5, 10, and 20 megabytes with 15 to 70 ms average access time.

The Back-up Problem

Because of their enormous storage capability as compared to traditional floppy disks, Winchester disk drives introduced a new problem: back-up storage. In case the Winchester disk drive should experience a malfunction or any accident, it is necessary to preserve a copy of the data contents on some other medium. The traditional answers in the computer world have been two: a removable disk pack, and tape drives. New tape drives designed as back-up units for Winchester disk drives are now available. Removable packs are not yet available but will probably become available in the future. A common back-up storage available today is a set of floppy disk drives. This implies that either the user selectively saves only those files that have been modified on the floppy disk, or uses a very powerful operating system capable of doing this automatically. If the entire contents of the hard disk were regularly dumped onto floppy disks, then the company using the system would soon be forced to move, as most of their file cabinets and rooms would be filled with diskettes. Floppy disks are not practical as a back-up medium because of their limited storage capability. However, they can be used if the user selects which files must be preserved, and keeps files reasonably small.

A preferred back-up system is a high-speed tape-drive: a complete disk can be backed-up on tape in a few minutes.

Winchester Summary

The main hardware limitation of microcomputers has been the limited amount of disk space. The new Winchester technology solves this problem at low cost. However, a Winchester disk must be backed-up on cartridge or tape. Winchester disks are still significantly slower than traditional fixed-head disks. In a business application involving significant file handling, the speed of the system will be disk-limited, and the expense of a traditional fixed-head disk may be justified. In all other cases, the new Winchester technology has removed the last significant technical limitation of microcomputers.

Even time-sharing systems that allow several terminals to share a common disk have now become practical.

Disk Summary

The floppy (or minifloppy) has become the standard mass storage device for microcomputers. A dual-drive is required for efficient operation. A minifloppy is adequate for personal computing. A floppy is the minimum required for business computing, while a Winchester disk is best for large business files.

TAPES

A home cassette recorder may be used as a low-cost mass storage medium. The home cassette recorder sacrifices the signal to noise ratio for low harmonic distortion (and ignores phase distortion), leading to reliability problems if a high encoding rate of bits per inch is used. *Caution:* a standard cassette recorder needs a remote ON/OFF connector, and must be unplugged during rewind or fast forward.

Digital cassette recorders also exist, but still have the disadvantages of a long access time, and sequential nature (no easy random access).

FUTURE BULK STORAGE

Two memory technologies have been developed that aim at providing a large amount of memory (such as one megabyte, which equals 1 million bytes) at high speed and low cost. They are: CCD (Charge-Coupled Devices) and bubble memory.

CCD may be a replacement for one minifloppy in a few years, but it is still volatile. Bubble memory may offer large permanent storage in a more distant future, but it is still expensive.

OTHER PERIPHERALS

The Light Pen

The light pen is an input device for use with a CRT display. It is a powerful and convenient communication device for pointing to a specific location on the screen. It works by simply sensing light when the area it is pointing to gets illuminated by the beam that continually scans the screen. The time at which the light is sensed allows the computer (or rather a program) to compute the approximate location on the screen.

The light pen is particularly convenient for selections: pointing it at a word on the screen allows for a rapid and convenient dialogue with a program by untrained personnel. However, it offers only limited precision, and should be used only to point to an area, not a specific dot on the screen. The light pen is expensive, and it is seldom used with microcomputers.

In a business environment: a light pen may not be convenient; the operator communicates with the system via the keyboard, and must confirm every selection. If the operator should accidentally point to the wrong selection on the screen, the entire selection procedure would need to be restarted to correct the error. With a keyboard, the program waits for a "Carriage Return" before executing, allowing time for verification or correction.

In an educational environment: the light pen is ideal, as an inexperienced user can dispense with using a keyboard, and errors are not so damaging. A child, for example, can point to the "correct" answer without knowing anything about keyboards.

The Joystick

The joystick is a vertical lever that can be moved left, right, forward, backward, or to any intermediate position. It is ideal for "moving a point across a screen quickly." It is used extensively for video games, and has a very low cost and low precision.

The Mouse

The mouse is the more precise version of the joystick. It is essentially a small device equipped with wheels, which can be moved by hand in all directions across a tablet. The motion of the wheels can be measured precisely, and a dot will be moved on the screen as the mouse is moved. Its name stems from a familiar nickname given to this device in view of its size and the type of motion used.

It is expensive, and usually not used with microcomputers.

The Tablet

Many types of digitized tablets exist, where one can essentially write or move a special "pen." The position of the pen is sensed, and correlated to a position on the screen. Good resolution results in a high price, so that tablets are seldom used with microcomputers.

Voice Input

Yes, it is possible to give verbal commands to a computer, with a suitable voice analyzer and its program. Within the range of prices compatible with microcomputers, such a system accepts a limited vocabulary (say a few dozen commands) of well-spoken short commands, after a "learning period" for each new user by the program. The processing time required may result in the order being executed only a few seconds after the command is spoken.

Such boards are commercially available, and may be added to a compatible system (generally S-100).

Voice Output

Voice can now be easily and inexpensively synthesized by special chips that produce an acceptable sounding voice in response to a specified encoding of phonemes (elementary speech units). Also, when a specific voice must be imitated, a synthesizer board can be used with a good analysis program that encodes the phonemes when spoken into a

Figure 9-23: "Speechlab" by Heuristics offers voice input, and is S-100 compatible.

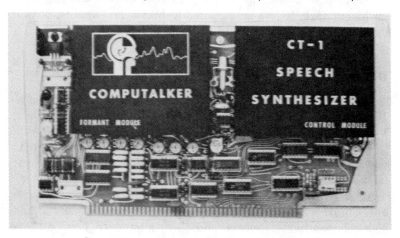

Figure 9-24: Computalker provides voice output

microphone, and a large program for the playback. The sound of the voice can be quite good. The main problem lies in good voice analysis, to correctly encode all of its features, so that manual "touch-up" may be necessary if a specific voice must be imitated.

OTHER DEVICES FOR PERSONAL SYSTEMS

LEDs

Light-Emitting Diodes are the least expensive display medium, but are limited to numerical digits or hexadecimal symbols (0 through 9, A through F) if they are to remain "low-cost." They are used on "one-board" microcomputers.

Switches

Sense switches can be connected directly to a microcomputer board, and are used for implementing home burglar alarms, or electric train automation.

Relays

Electromechanical relays provide a convenient isolation between two circuits. Miniature relays can now be mounted directly on the microcomputer board, allowing you to close a circuit carrying a substantial voltage. Relays are required to turn lights, motors, or other devices on or off.

DACs and ADCs

Measuring a voltage with a digital voltmeter will display, for example, 12.5V. The voltage is an analog (continuously varying) quantity. 12.5V is a digitized value, giving the approximate measurement with a .1V precision. A DAC is a Digital-to-Analog Converter, required if you want your computer to produce an analog signal that can vary (almost continuously).

An ADC is an Analog-to-Digital Converter, and was required by our voltmeter. An ADC is needed for the measurement of any physical quantity: temperature, pressure, or intensity. Low-cost, one-chip ADCs are now available.

SUMMARY

A number of options exist for specialized facilities. However, a brief summary is the following:
1. A minimal personal system needs: a microcomputer, a keyboard, a CRT monitor (or TV), and a tape cassette
2. A better system will use a minifloppy instead of a cassette
3. A business system requires: a microcomputer with large internal memory, CRT terminal with business keyboard, two full-sized floppy disks, and/or one or more Winchester disks, and a printer with a pin feed mechanism.

In conclusion:
— Every microcomputer system uses a keyboard and a CRT
— Almost every system uses a cassette recorder or a disk
— Most systems require a printer

The analysis of characteristics and peripherals presented in this chapter should serve as an important practical guideline for the selection of the peripherals. In most systems, they will represent the major cost.

10

SELECTING A MICROCOMPUTER

INTRODUCTION

This chapter describes typical microcomputers in each of the three different categories: single-board, integrated unit, and general-purpose. Of course, because of the rapid change in the technology, no such list can ever be considered complete. The computers shown in this section are therefore intended to illustrate the advantages and disadvantages of the various designs.

A brief history of computers will retrace the appearance of the first personal computer. Then, personal computers will be classified into three categories. Finally, a number of typical systems will be described in each category, and the criteria for selection will be summarized.

A MICRO-HISTORY OF COMPUTERS

Scientific computation for applications such as astronomy, navigation, geographical measurements, and record-keeping dates back thousands of years. In fact, the ancient Chinese abacus is an example of early efforts to mechanize simple computing tasks.

The next important step on the path toward automation of computing was Pascal's mechanical adder (1643, France). It was invented by the young Pascal to facilitate accounting, and used moving wheels with cogs, so that each transition from "9" to "0" would trigger the next wheel to the left (this is now called "adding a carry").

The next conceptual step was Babbage's work on his "analytical engine" (1820's to 1834, Great Britain). Widely regarded as an eccentric, Babbage could not get his model implemented, but had, in fact, defined a model of today's general-purpose computer. His work was in advance of his time and not understood.

1890 marked the beginning of automation, with the development of Hollerith's punched card, followed by automated card counting. This work was directed at solving the problem of U.S. census tabulation, and the product marked the entry of a company known as IBM into the data processing field.

Next came the introduction of the first computers at the end of World War II (1944-45). The MARK I was developed by Howard Aiken at Harvard with IBM funding, while the ENIAC was developed by Eckart and Mauchly with U.S. Army funding at the Moore School of the University of Pennsylvania.

The MARK I was a "first-generation computer" using electro-mechanical relays, which operated from 1944 to 1959.

The ENIAC (Electronic Numerical Integrator and Computer) was a "second-generation computer" using vacuum tubes (18,000 of them). The ENIAC operated from 1946 to 1958. This huge machine was built for computing trajectories of missiles. Programming changes required days, as they involved rewiring and resoldering. The "stored program" computer had not yet been invented. The ENIAC filled a large room at the Moore School of Electrical Engineering and only worked for a few hours between failures. The ENIAC had only 1K bits of working memory (vs. 16K or more for a contemporary micro-computer), used 10,000 capacitors, 65,000 resistors, and 7,300 relays or switches. It weighed 65,000 pounds and filled 3,000 cubic feet. The power required was 160 kilowatts.

At this point IBM examined the results, decided that computers had no future, and did not pursue the market.

In 1945, Von Neumann finally formulated the concept of a stored program computer, where both program and data are stored in a memory, allowing complete generality in executing any program. ENIAC was then to be followed by a number of "---ACs" (Automatic Computers):

— EDVAC (Electronic Discrete Variable Automatic Computer)
— EDSAC (Electronic Delay Storage Automatic Computer)
— UNIVAC (UNIVersal Automatic Computer) created in 1951 by Eckart and Mauchly for the U.S. Census Bureau.

IBM then realized that it had wrongly assessed the future of computers. The 701 was introduced in 1953, and succeeded in capturing a large share of the market.

Transistors became a reality in the late fifties and caused the introduction of "third-generation" computers.

1964-66 was marked by three notable events. IBM introduced the 360 line, which gave the company its world-wide domination. DEC (Digital Equipment Corporation) introduced the PDP 6, followed by the PDP 8, the most successful minicomputer. At the other end of the spectrum, CDC (Control Data Corporation) introduced the CDC 6600, a "super-computer" for the most complex numerical computations.

The Fourth Generation

In the early 1960's the area around Sunnyvale, at the south end of the San Francisco Bay, was still a peaceful agricultural area, known for its orchards. It has now become an extended industrial park known as "Silicon Valley." This is where a majority of the semiconductor manufacturers are established. Throughout the 1960's, it became possible to integrate an ever-increasing number of transistors and other components on a single chip of silicon, until, in the early 1970's, several thousand transistors could be realized on a chip; this was the era of LSI (Large Scale Integration). Such a number of transistors makes it possible to implement a simplified computer, or rather its CPU, on a chip.

In November 1971, the 4004 microprocessor was announced by Intel. At that time, Intel was a small company in Silicon Valley. More than a year passed before Intel and the other semiconductor manufacturers realized that a revolutionary new component had been introduced by accident. Most of the leading microprocessors known today were then introduced: the Intel 8080, Motorola 6800, Zilog Z80, MOS Technology 6502, etc.

However, all the applications of microprocessors were in the computer field, in industrial control, or avionics. Just like computers at their beginning, microprocessors were used for "scientific" purposes, rather than for data processing. As yet, no one had fully realized their potential.

The next significant event occured in January 1975, with the announcement of the Altair personal computer by MITS, then a small company in New Mexico. In the years that followed, microcomputer companies sprang up across the country to satisfy this new market. Most could not deliver enough units; some still cannot. A detailed survey of the products available is presented in this chapter.

MICROCOMPUTER TYPES

The criteria for selecting a microcomputer CPU and peripherals have been presented in the preceding chapters. They can now be applied to actual systems, in order to evaluate their advantages and disadvantages.

Two main packaging formats have been differentiated thus far:
1. The single-board microcomputer
2. The microcomputer system

Two additional packaging formats can now be distinguished for micro-computer systems:

1. The "integrated" microcomputer
2. The "general-purpose" system

The integrated microcomputer includes the keyboard and the micro-computer in the same box. This type of packaging is used for low-cost, home-use systems. The advantages are: ease in handling, lower enclosure cost, and pleasing appearance. The usual disadvantages are the lack of room in the enclosure and lack of sufficient power supply for future expansion (such as additional memory or interface boards).

The general-purpose system has an enclosure that allows for expansion to 64K memory, as well as disk and printer interfaces.

The three categories above will now be surveyed.

Caution: because of the rapid rate of introduction of new systems (and the retirement of some), this survey does not claim to be complete. Prices and technical characteristics change rapidly. This analysis is presented for its educational value.

SINGLE-BOARD MICROCOMPUTERS

The limitations of single-board microcomputers have already been pointed out. Outside of the engineering and control fields, their essential value lies in learning elementary programming or interfacing techniques. Most microprocessor manufacturers offer a single-board microcomputer equipped with a minimal keyboard and four to six LEDs, which can be used for such purposes at a minimal cost.

Several single-board microcomputers have been designed specifically as low-cost educational tools, with on-board keyboard and LEDs. They deserve a brief mention here.

The KIM-1 and the SYM-1

Originally introduced by MOS Technology (now a division of Commodore), the KIM-1 is now also available from Rockwell International. An "improved" KIM-1 has been announced as the SYM-1 by Synertek (a second-source of the 6502 microprocessor used in the KIM).

The KIM-1 has on board: 1K RAM, two 6530 ROM-RAM-I/O combinations (equal to 2K ROM), a 23-key keyboard, six LEDs, as well as the interfaces for a Teletype, and a standard cassette recorder.

To use the KIM, the user simply needs a power supply. To use a tape recorder, the user only needs to connect Audio In, Audio Out. The connection to a Teletype is just as simple.

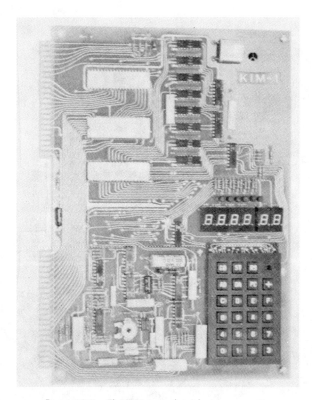

Figure 10-1:   The KIM-1 one-board microcomputer

The SYM-1 has an additional I/O port, and a number of additional features.

The AIM-65

The AIM-65 from Rockwell is analogous to the SYM-1, but offers a one-line display and a micro-printer on a single board. It is one of the least-expensive tools for learning assembly language.

NEC TK80

A compact single-board microcomputer, the TK80 has been designed as a training tool for learning the 8080A (also manufactured by NEC in Japan). It is equipped with a hexadecimal keyboard, plus nine keys for monitor commands, and eight LEDs for display.

A portion of the board is left free for user breadboarding. ROM/

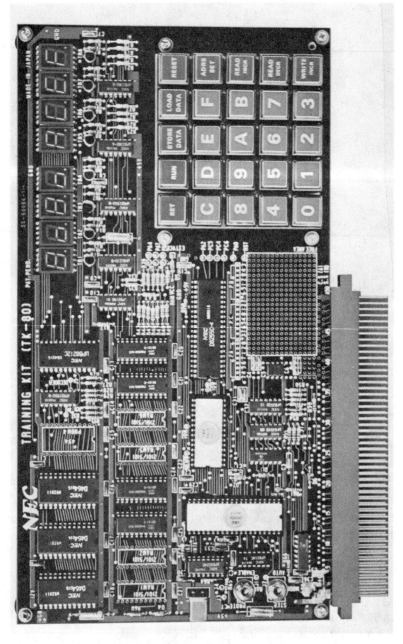

Figure 10-2: Nippon electronic single-board microcomputer

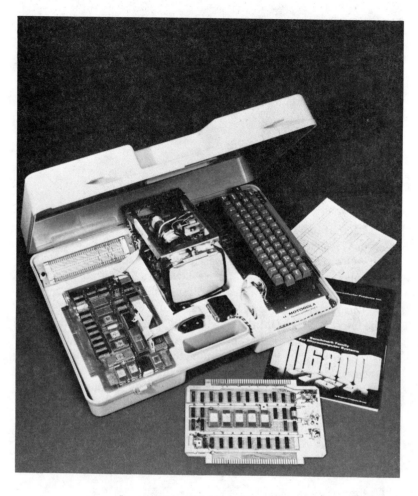

Figure 10-3:   A "kit" from Motorola

PROM and RAM are expandable—up to 1K bytes on board. The
manufacturer-supplied monitor resides in ROM addresses 0000 to
02FF (755 bytes). RAM battery back-up is also available.

INTEGRATED SYSTEMS

Integrated systems are targeted at less than $1000 for a complete,
usable system (including a display and tape recorder), and can often
be purchased for much less. Let us observe some typical examples.

Personal Computers

The PET, TRS80, Atari, Exidy, and Apple are integrated systems designed as low-cost personal computers. All supply BASIC in ROM. These, and others, are presented below.

Commodore PET/CBM

Characteristics:
— *Microprocessor used: 6502*
— *Integrated keyboard and CRT*
— *IEEE 488 interface (no RS-232 connector)*
— *Limited graphics capability (64 graphic characters)*

PET stands for "Personal Electronic Transactor," and is a complete integrated system, with its own display. Programs may be loaded from cassettes, or from other peripherals, through the IEEE 488 interface. It is equipped with full alphanumeric keyboard, featuring 64 graphic characters (see illustration), and has upper-case and lower-case letters (however, graphics and lower-case are mutually exclusive).

The internal 14K ROM includes: BASIC interpreter (8K), operating system (4K), diagnostic routine (1K), and machine language monitor (1K). The BASIC interpreter is complete, providing ten-digit floating character addressing (PEEK and POKE commands).

A possible disadvantage is the lack of an RS-232 connector, which restricts the peripherals that may be easily attached to the unit.

Typical uses: games, education, home finance, simple business applications.

Radio Shack TRS-80 Model I

Characteristics:
— *Microprocessor used: Z-80*
— *Standard memory: 4K ROM, 4K RAM. Internally expandable to 12K ROM and 16K RAM*
— *Keyboard: 53-key, typewriter style. Business keyboard available.*
— *Graphics: 128 horizontal by 48 vertical*
— *Special I/O expansion port.*

A direct competitor of the PET, this is also a complete system, with (detached) keyboard, CRT monitor, and tape cassette. Peripherals must be connected through the proprietary expansion port, on the back of the keyboard/computer case. Most require the use of an

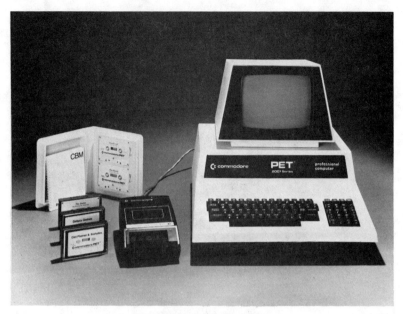

Figure 10-4:   Standard PET

Figure 10-5:   PET 8000 series features a wide screen (80 columns).

Figure 10-6:   Radio Shack TRS-80 Model I

Figure 10-7:   TRS-80 Model II is business-oriented.

"expansion unit." "Level II BASIC" is a complete BASIC, and there is an assembler for machine language programming.

Its keyboard is a standard "QWERTY" typewriter keyboard, through which all commands are entered. The microcomputer is contained in the keyboard enclosure.

Typical uses: games, education, limited business (payroll), and general-purpose finance.

Figure 10-8:   The Apple II has color video output.

Apple II

Characteristics:
— *Microprocessor used: 6502*
— *Standard memory: 8K ROM (includes BASIC), 4K RAM, expandable to 48K RAM internally.*
— *Keyboard: 52-key, typewriter style*
— *I/O: color TV output (RF), 24 lines × 40 characters (5 × 7 upper case characters). Graphics capability: 280 horizontal by 192 vertical, in four colors. Includes cassette interface, speaker, and paddle connectors.*

Because of the integrated keyboard, this unit is similar in appearance to games-oriented computers. However, it offers in-box expansion to 48K bytes of RAM (on the single board), and two additional ROM sockets. As a result, it has full computing capability, without any memory limitation.

The Apple II requires an external TV, and includes the color interface, as well as a standard cassette interface, and paddle interfaces.

The 8K ROM includes a 2K "monitor" (with mini-assembler, disassembler, debugger, floating-point package) plus a 6K BASIC with some limitations (integers only from -32767 to $+32767$ and single dimensional arrays.)

Characters are limited to upper-case.

Typical uses: color TV games, general-purpose computing.

Special interface boards for serial output (printers) or disks plug directly into the enclosure.

Although this is an integrated system, it has the same capabilities as a general-purpose system: it can be connected to the usual peripherals, and equipped with additional memory, without any additional "expansion box." This is a significant convenience.

The new Apple III has been designed to offer general-purpose business capabilities.

Exidy Sorcerer

Technical characteristics:
— *Microprocessor used: Z80*
— *Integrated keyboard and microcomputer*
— *Integrated CRT and floppy disk (2 mini-floppies)*
— *ROM cartridges*

Atari

Technical characteristics:
— *Microprocessor used: 6502*
— *Integrated keyboard and microcomputer*
— *External monitor or TV required*
— *Two models: 400 and 800*
— *ROM cartridges available*
— *Video output: B&W on 400, color on 800*
Noted for its excellent games.

Figure 10-9: The Exidy Sorcerer is a fully integrated unit.

Figure 10-10: The Atari low-cost model connects to black and white TV

Figure 10-11: The Atari model 800 has color graphics

Ohio Scientific Challenger C1P and C4P

Technical characteristics:
— *Microprocessor used: 6502*
— *Integrated keyboard*
— *Model 1P has black and white video output, Model 4P has color.*
— *C4P has four slots (one available).*

Texas Instruments 99/4

Technical characteristics:
— *Uses TI microprocessor*
— *Integrates keyboard and cassette recorder*
— *16K RAM memory*
— *Color video output (external monitor or TV required — 13-inch monitor optional)*
— *Sound and graphics (16 colors)*
— *Optional speech synthesizer*
-- *"Solid State Software" modules available from TI (ROM memory)*

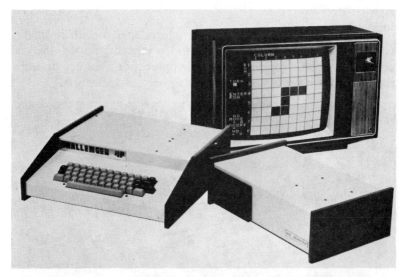

Figure 10-12:   Ohio Scientific Challenger connects to TV

Figure 10-13:   TI 99/4 has color video output.

Hewlett-Packard HP-85

This microcomputer is a completely integrated unit, with keyboard, CRT display (high resolution), cartridge tape drive, and thermal printer. It uses a proprietary HP microprocessor, and has been designed for professional users, such as engineers and scientists.

Figure 10-14:   HP85 integrates everything, including the printer.

Figure 10-15:   I/O modules plug into the back of HP/85.

IBM 5120

This desk-top computer has both BASIC and APL in ROM. It is priced higher than most integrated computers.

Figure 10-16: IBM 5120 has APL and BASIC in ROM.

GENERAL-PURPOSE COMPUTERS

Many of the early computers that dominated the field at the beginning have now disappeared: IMSAI, Processor Technology, and the Digital Group. Only a few have survived, and more changes are likely to occur. Many, but not all, use the S-100 bus, which is no longer as prevalent as it was with early microcomputers. All of the leading brands offer extensive software support with languages such as BASIC, PASCAL, and sometimes FORTRAN and COBOL, as well as applications software: word processing, mailing list and accounting. Specific software availability and ease of connecting required peripherals (specific printers or disks, for example) generally represent the major criteria for selection.

Most computers using the 8080 or the Z80 support the CP/M operating system, thereby offering a wide range of software. General-purpose computers now tend to be used in situations where an expensive minicomputer had to be used in the past.

Altair 8800-b

Technical characteristics:
— *Microcomputer used: 8080*
— *Standard memory: Any amount of ROM/RAM, up to 64K*
— *I/O: RS-232, 20mA current loop. Serial I/O port.*
— *Features integrated front-panel (optional). 16 additional S-100 boards possible in basic box.*

The Altair is included for historical reasons: it was the first microcomputer introduced, and is a general-purpose computer. It created the S-100 bus, now an industry standard. The basic box could be custom-specified as to its card-contents. A variety of boards are available: memories, interfaces, and special-purpose.

To be used, this microcomputer box must be connected to a CRT terminal (with a keyboard), a mass memory (such as a disk), and, optimally, a printer. Altair is now part of Pertec Computers.

Cromemco

Characteristics:
— *Microprocessor used: Z80 A (4MHz version)*
— *Memory: 1K PROM, 32K to 64K RAM*
— *I/O: RS-232 plus 8-bit parallel interface*
— *Uses S-100 bus. 21 board slots*

The "System Three" has high-quality packaging, and incorporates two full-sized floppies, with room for two more. It is available with a Winchester disk.

Figure 10-17: A typical Cromemco system

North-Star Horizon

Characteristics:
— *Microprocessor used: Z-80A (4MHz version)*
— *Memory expandable to 64K*
— *S-100 bus. Integrated dual mini-floppy drives*
— *Optional floating-point unit for fast arithmetic.*
A Winchester disk is also available.

Figure 10-18: North Star integrates two mini-floppies.

Ohio Scientific C3-C

Technical characteristics:
— *Has three microprocessors: 6502, Z80 and 6800*
— *One of the first systems to integrate a Winchester disk.*

Figure 10-19:   Ohio Scientific C3-C features hard disks.

Vector MZ

Technical characteristics:
— *Microprocessor used: Z80*
— *Integrates two mini-floppies.*

Figure 10-20:   Vector MZ integrates two mini-floppies.

Polymorphic 88

Characteristics:
— *Microprocessor used: 8080*
— *Memory: 3K ROM, 16K RAM, expandable to 64K*
— *Features: S-100 bus (5 slots). Several packaging options available.*

Altos ACS8000-6

— *Uses the Z80. Designed for CP/M operation.*

Compucolor II

Characteristics:
— *Microprocessor used: 8080A*
— *Memory: 16K ROM, 8K RAM (includes 4K RAM refresh), expandable to 32K ROM, 32K RAM*
— *I/O: integrated color CRT (13-inch), 32 lines × 64 characters optional standard ASCII keyboard. Integrated mini-floppy. RS-232C port*
— *Features: Vector software, 64 special characters*

This system provides both general-purpose computing and limited color graphics.

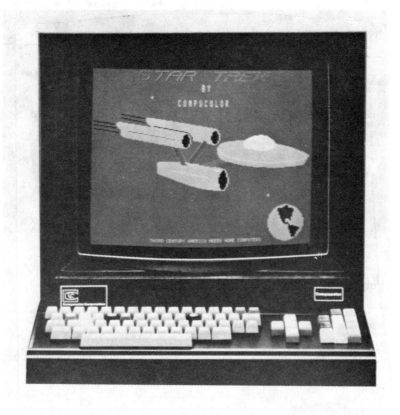

Figure 10-21: Compucolor has an integral color screen. This model has a separate disk.

Digital Equipment PDP 11/03

Characteristics:
— *Microprocessor used: LSI-11 chip set*
— *Memory: 4K, expandable to 64K*
— *Features: compatible with PDP11 line instruction set. Excellent software. Up to six additional modules in the enclosure.*

This microcomputer was developed by DEC as a lower-cost replacement of the 11/05 minicomputer, and originally used the Western Digital chip set (the LSI-11). This system is usable as a personal computer, but has been essentially marketed with DECs mainline, i.e., in the laboratory and control markets.

Like all the PDP11 line, it has extensive software, in particular, Dartmouth BASIC, ANSI, FORTRAN, and RT-11, a real time operating system with simultaneous foreground/background operations.

OTHER MANUFACTURERS

Other important manufacturers include SWTPC (6800-based computers), Zenith Data Systems (formerly Heathkit), Dynabyte (with the Z80 microprocessor), Alpha-Micro Systems (uses a 16-bit design analogous to the LSI-11, and is S-100 bus-compatible), Onyx (with the Z8000 microprocessor), and many more that cannot be listed here.

Figure 10-22:   ONYX is based on Z8000, a 16-bit microprocessor

SUMMARY

Three types of microcomputers have been distinguished: single-board (education), integrated system (games, education, limited business use), and general-purpose (all applications).

Typical products have been presented for each type. The major criteria for selection of the different systems are:

For personal use: integrated systems offer high computing capability at a very modest cost. Their primary disadvantage stems from the difficulty and cost of expansion. If the possible technical limitations and software of integrated systems are sufficient for an application, then they represent the best choice. Integrated systems tend to be used in situations where a computer has not been used before.

Additional criteria are cost, color, graphics, and (most important), the availability of the required software.

For scientific use: integrated systems are well-suited for scientific and engineering applications. A low-cost system can be dedicated to scientific computations or laboratory automation, as it offers high computing power at minimal cost. Large files are usually not required, so there is no need for expensive disks or printers.

For business use: integrated systems are often adequate for limited business applications. However, in most cases, a general-purpose system with disks and a printer is required. The availability of the necessary peripherals and the required software is the most important criterion. Both should be of proven quality. A Winchester disk with adequate back-up is often desirable.

11

ECONOMICS OF A BUSINESS SYSTEM

THE REAL COST OF A SYSTEM

It is possible today to acquire a minimal system for as little as $150 to $500, including the power supply, and minimal input-output devices.

If your intent is to do some "serious programming," or to execute business programs, it will usually be necessary to:

1. Add memory
2. Add a CRT terminal
3. Add one or more disks (if not included)
4. Add a printèr (almost never included).

Starting with a $1000 to $2000 microcomputer box, the total price of the system will be perhaps four times the cost of the box, or even more, in the case of the business system (with the addition of the cost of software).

This has always been true of computer systems. For a complete system, the principal cost is that of the peripherals.

Although the cost of electronic components will still decrease, the cost of the peripherals is not likely to decrease significantly, unless a new mass market appears.

The Hidden Costs

Two main additional cost factors must be added to the purchase cost of a system: maintenance and programming.

In the case of a business system, a rule of thumb is to estimate maintenance at 1% of purchase cost per month.

Programming is not a significant cost in the case of a personal system; it is either done for enjoyment, or else programs can be purchased at a low cost.

In the case of a business system, standard business packages are just that: they are standardized, and will never exactly fit the need of every business, especially small businesses, which tend to be highly individualized.

It is common practice to schedule at least a half-time programmer as part of the permanent cost of a computer system. The programmer will be responsible for adapting the standard programs and developing the specialized packages required by the business.

A third additional hidden cost stems from the impact of computerized procedures on a business. In the ideal case, the computer will eliminate the need for several job positions, or significantly simplify many tasks.

In practice, this is not always the case. In a small company, the computer is unlikely to eliminate any job. The bookkeeper will still be needed, as well as the sales clerk. The computer, however, will automate some of their tasks, saving some time, but, more importantly, providing new resources:

—Instantaneous reports and updates
—Inventory management
—Immediate statistics.

More of the time of valuable personnel will be free for more complex tasks, and all repetitive work is likely to be performed much more accurately: sales reports, overdue notices, automatic reorder. In a growth situation, the microcomputer is likely to eliminate the need for additional clerical personnel, resulting in salary savings. Finally, the availability of up-to-date information also has significant management value.

In short, in all cases where the previous criteria are met, i.e., growth or high value of immediate information, a computer will result in immediate savings.

In other cases, its use may not be necessary unless other services are valued, such as mailing list management.

When to Buy

Let P indicate the purchase price of the system.

Let M be the maintenance cost.

Let A be any additional costs (programmer or other).

The cost of the system is:

$$P + (M + A) \times T$$

where T is the time (in months).

In fact, one should add L = one-time loss of time incurred when the system is installed, and the transition is made.

The total cost is now: $P + (M + A) \times T + L$.

On the positive side, the computer may be assumed to save D dollars per month by reducing the payroll, and eliminating external data processing services (mailing list, payroll).

If D is small, the system will not "pay for itself" unless one takes into consideration the dollar value of additional services it provides.

If D is significant, the system will have paid for itself when the cost of the system has been compensated by savings, i.e., when:

$$P + (M + A) \times T + L = D \times T$$

that is, after a time $T = \dfrac{P + L}{D - M - A}$

In order to break even after 18 months, for example, the monthly savings D must be:

$$D = \frac{P + L + (M + A) \times 18}{18}$$

Finally, D should include not only the payroll savings and external EDP savings but should also take into account the additional income generated by the availability of:
— Up-to-date reports
— Immediate reorder (no loss in profits due to delay)
— Improved marketing through analysis and mailings
— Improved collection of receivables.

The formula proposed is therefore likely to be a "worst possible case."

In addition, the educational value of the process will result in substantial savings a few years later, when the business has grown.

Are There Options?

The traditional options to the in-house system are:
1. External data processing service
2. Rental of a time-sharing terminal.
Let us examine these two options.

External Data Processing

External data processing may be economical for highly specialized tasks: payroll, taxes, mailing list. However, it has disadvantages:

costs, reliability, turn-around time increasing with the growth of the business, lack of information security, and accessibility. External EDP is still a viable alternative for many businesses that would derive only limited benefits from an in-house computer. In fact, service businesses are appearing that use microcomputers to provide these specialized services to a group of users.

Discipline

Possibly the most important single source of "computer malfunction" is the lack of proper discipline by the operator. The main recommendations can be summarized as follows:
— Set all switches correctly at all times, especially on the printer.
— Handle diskettes gently and correctly. Keep them away from dust and magnetic sources.
— Follow all instructions for hardware and software use strictly. No exceptions should be made until you are aware of all possible consequences.

Disciplined computer users experience very few failures. Sloppy or undisciplined users are usually responsible for most "computer failures."

Time-Sharing

It is possible to rent a terminal (CRT or printer) and communicate via a telephone line with a central computer. The user pays for the rental of the terminal, the line, the connection time, and the processing time used. This option is very convenient: one is connected to a powerful computer, equipped with all facilities. However, this is an expensive alternative: the cost of renting or buying a terminal with a modem is a substantial proportion of the cost of a microcomputer.

Unless highly specialized processing is needed (or else access to the computer is free), an in-house system, provided that it can supply the required service, is now usually more economical.

SUMMARY

The cost benefit trade-offs of a microcomputer system have been analyzed and evaluated. In most growing businesses, the threshold of computer profitability is likely to be reached quickly. Provided that the capital is available, early computerization can become a significant asset. Finally, provided that due care is exercised, the financial risks are small.

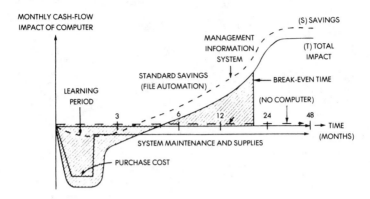

MONTHLY CASH-FLOW
IMPACT OF COMPUTER

(S) SAVINGS

MANAGEMENT
INFORMATION
SYSTEM

(T) TOTAL
IMPACT

STANDARD SAVINGS
(FILE AUTOMATION)

BREAK-EVEN TIME

LEARNING
PERIOD

(NO COMPUTER)

3   6   12   24   48   TIME
(MONTHS)

SYSTEM MAINTENANCE AND SUPPLIES

PURCHASE COST

Figure 11-1:   The profitability curve of a computer system

12

HOW TO FAIL
WITH A BUSINESS SYSTEM

INTRODUCTION

The word "failure" will define those system problems that are "accidental," i.e., due to error. This chapter will explore the sources of error. Every user of a business system should be aware of these pitfalls, in order to avoid them.

The basic guideline for all of the comments to be presented is that a business system should be secure and reliable. Failures will be traced to three essential sources: hardware, software, and procedures.

HARDWARE FAILURES

We will assume that the system has been delivered in good operating condition. The first 100 to 200 hours of operation are called the *burn-in* period. It is during this period that bad components are most likely to fail. Many manufacturers or retailers will "burn-in" a unit prior to shipment.

Let us now consider the hardware failures most likely to occur 'hroughout the life of the equipment.

Mechanical Failures

Mechanical failures are usually the most likely to occur, and the most common source of mechanical failure is the printer. To forestall such failures, preventive maintenance is normally used in a production environment: mechanical parts are inspected, cleaned, and adjusted every x hours. This procedure catches most malfunctions before they occur.

The next most likely cause of failure is a damaged diskette. This is almost always due to incorrect handling.

Environmental Failures

All components of a system are rated within a specified temperature range and humidity level. Clearly, these specifications must be met. However, malfunctions due to temporary non-compliance are usually transient, and will not damage the system permanently.

Electronic Failures

As in any complex system, some of the electronic components might malfunction. The general recommendation is to leave the diagnosis and repair to the supplier.

Summary of Hardware Failures

Provided the system is built according to generally accepted guidelines for reliable operation, or is reputed to be reliable, hardware malfunctions are likely to be minimal after the first few days. They are normally entrusted to the manufacturer's repair service, or to the local supplier. It is of critical importance for a business system that local on-site service be available.

SOFTWARE FAILURES

Every complex program should be deemed incorrect! At least in the mathematical sense, as there will almost always be some combination of events that will cause the program to malfunction. However, the probability is small, and, generally little damage will result.

Because there is no way to guarantee that any long program, like any complex man-built system, is totally error-free, every system will occasionally suffer from software bugs. Traditionally, manufacturers release periodic updates of programs where significant bugs have been found. For example, almost every BASIC interpreter, when first released, will misbehave when some specific sequence of instructions is used. These problems are later corrected.

Any software that has not yet been tested by a large number of users must be assumed to contain bugs. Any new software facility should, therefore, be treated cautiously in a business environment.

The point, however, should not be overstated; some users may never notice significant malfunctions. The system may not accept a command, and it will simply have to be retyped. If good system design is used, the malfunctions are often limited to the need to repeat an operation that did not work.

Even the largest IBM systems experience catastrophic "crashes" on occasion. In fact, because of their very complexity, they are more likely to malfunction and require a number of reliability enhancement techniques.

SPECIAL TECHNIQUES FOR ENHANCED RELIABILITY

Parity has long been a favorite technique for verifying the correct transmission or retention of information. Parity consists of adding an extra bit to each byte of data to verify its contents. *Even* parity will add a "zero" if the total number of ones in the byte is even, otherwise, it will add a "one." In other words, even parity guarantees that the total number of bits will be even. *Odd* parity may also be used.

This technique will detect "single bit failures" that are the most likely to occur: if a single bit changes state, the parity verification module will compare the computed parity bit to the one stored with the byte, and detect the failure.

Parity is used extensively in medium and large scale systems. It is almost never used in microcomputers for two reasons:
1. Microprocessor systems are much more reliable than even traditional minicomputers, simply because they use far fewer components (the failure rate increases with the number of parts and interconnections).
2. There has been no demand thus far for the additional reliability, at extra cost and complexity.

One of the areas where a malfunction is likely to occur is the memory of the system, primarily because it uses a large number of components. A temporary failure during a space war game is not objectionable: the game is just restarted. A temporary failure that wipes out hours of accounts receivable data has a more serious consequence, however.

Since business systems are likely to require the largest RAM memory available (48 or 64K bytes), memory malfunctions are also more likely to occur. There may soon be memory systems for microprocessors equipped with the parity option, in order to provide the extra reliability.

Parity is used at the byte level. However, in mass memories such as a disk or tape, it is not possible to dedicate an extra bit to this function. In this case, an entire byte (or several bytes) is used at the end of specified blocks. This byte contains a *checksum* or a *CRC (cyclic redundancy check)*.

The checksum is computed according to a simple formula involving the previous n bytes (where "n" depends upon the system). If a byte is changed, the checksum is changed. The checksum verification module will then detect it when the block of data is read. CRC uses a more complex technique for computing the CRC bytes.

Checksum or CRC are universally used in the case of disks or tapes. The checksum is a simplified method, while the CRC is a more reliable one.

Finally, another good practice is the *read after write:* whenever a block of data is written, it should be read again. This is sometimes done in the case of disks, and should be used for crucial files. Read after write is a software function that is usually not implemented, as it slows down the write operation. Its availability as an option may be valuable.

PROCEDURES

Several areas must be distinguished, as this is probably the area to which most serious failures can be traced.

Because it is difficult to strictly separate some procedures from their software implementation, many software aspects will also be discussed here.

Operator Discipline

The computer operator should always follow the proper rules for installation, including rules about hardware and software use.
— Diskettes should always be handled with proper care
— All settings on the printer should be correct
— No ventilation outlets should be obstructed
— Create a back-up copy at the end of every day on disk, tape or paper, so that any damaged or lost file may be recreated.
— Protect yourself against power fluctuations if the problem affects your area.

Data Accuracy

Data should be verified when entered, so that accuracy is retained when processed by the computer. In many cases, this can be done by field checks and limit checks. A *field check* verifies, for example, that a "number" does not accidentally contain characters, or two periods. A *limit check* is also called a "reasonableness test." For example, a number, used to indicate a month should be between 1 and 12. An unusually large or small entry should be detected. A traditional computer horror story is the following: an inexperienced (or tired) typist in a government office enters a $1,000,000 order in the accounts receivable file, instead of $10,000. The manager has approved an expenditure rate of 30% of receivables. Before the error is caught, up to $300,000 could be spent.

Another possible horror story is the "Mr. Smith case." A $780 payment is received from Mr. Smith. It is promptly credited to his account, which showed a balance of only $180 due. A $600 refund check is issued. One month later, an irate Mr. Smith calls in, and asks why he is receiving a computerized "final notice" when he paid in full. You guessed why. There were two "Mr. Smiths" in the file. The payment was credited to the wrong one.

Either a human or a software procedure should check for this situation. Ideally, the program will flag the "multiple Smiths."

Enforcing Controls

A general business principle is that duties should be separated: the person verifying data should not be the one entering them. This reduces the risk of accidental errors and also introduces a control against malicious modifications.

Also, from a procedural standpoint, it is a vital business practice to maintain an *audit trail* within all files: simply, all files and transactions must include appropriate references to the source files or documents that will allow a verification.

A simple example is, that at a minimum, a payment must be correlated to a date, check number, and invoice number. Similarly, a commission list must be correlated to the transactions from which the commissions originated.

In other items, sufficient cross-references must be listed to allow the complete verification of all data.

Check Digits

In situations where long codes are used (e.g., with inventories), it is essential to use either redundant encoding, or check digits.

Redundant encoding uses codes such as:

```
TUBE - 204211
BOLT - 418182
ASBL - 881921
FRME - 329137
```

The letters at the beginning of the code identify the product for a human operator. Every "tube" has a "204" code. Every "bolt" has a "418" code. The program checks that the code matches the letters. At most, errors will occur within the various tube or bolt types available, i.e., within the last three digits. This method is easy to implement but wastes space.

A *check digit* is an extra digit added to the code that detects transposition or single digit errors.

For example, 881921-5:

"5" is the "check digit." It is computed by multiplying "1" by n, then "2" by n^2, then "9" by n^2, etc., and then adding up the six numbers. The sum is divided by n. If the remainder is R, the check digit is $n - R$. The choice of n varies. This method is almost always used on checking account numbers, as the most frequent error is a transposition, i.e., writing 21224138 instead of 21221438.

Data Security

Files should be secure both in the event of machine malfunctions, and in the case of human error or interference. Of course, all important files should be duplicated at regular intervals, and safeguarded. Software safeguards, such as passwords or other access protection mechanisms, should also be available from a good file system.

A *password* can be imposed for a specific access to a file, such as Read or Write. It must not be echoed, and must not be easily accessible within the system. Once created, a file can thus be protected against unauthorized access or modification by the wrong person.

File protection features associated with a good file system are the ability to specify "access attributes" associated with a file, such as "write-protect."

Finally, simple means such as a key on the terminal should not be underestimated.

Computer-Shock

The effects of computerizing can be severe. Usually, unless the operating personnel have been adequately trained for the transition, significant processing delays may occur initially, resulting in lower performance for a period of time. However, there is normally a quick transition to higher efficiency, provided that correct procedures are implemented.

SUMMARY

Limited hardware and software failures must be expected. If all of the precautions indicated are taken, they should not significantly affect the operation of the system.

The greatest risk is usually in the procedures (both programmed and managerial) used with the new system. Common sense, sound business judgement, and advice from an experienced user are the basic required resources.

BUYING THE SYSTEM—A SUMMARY

1. There must be a need. The nature and amount of work must justify the change. This can be measured by the number of identical transactions or reports to be generated. In addition, the computer system may be justified by the unique problems that it may solve in special situations, such as inventory management, mailing lists, and management reports.
2. When to buy? Prices for electronics continue to decrease every year, while prices for peripherals tend to stabilize or decrease slowly. Tomorrow's system will always be cheaper than today's. However, if a computer system means savings of N dollars per month, then deferring its installation by m months is equivalent to a loss of $m \times N$ dollars.
3. Which to buy? All of the main options and equipment available have been presented.

13

HELP

OBTAINING INFORMATION

Many sources of information now exist that will facilitate decisions:

—Publications
—Clubs
—Computer stores
—Consultants
—Educational institutions or companies

The major new sources will now be reviewed.

MAGAZINES

Most of the traditional electronics or computer magazines feature regular articles on microcomputers. However, a number of new publications have emerged since 1976 that are designed specifically for the user or designer of microcomputers. They are listed at the end of this chapter. It is difficult to assign them to a specific field, as their contents evolve continuously. However, *"Dr. Dobb's Journal"* and *"Creative Computing"* always contain a substantial software selection, while *"Interface Age," "Byte,"* and *"Kilobaud"* also contain hardware designs. Many of these magazines are available at newsstands.

CLUBS AND COMPUTER STORES

A number of hobbyist's clubs have appeared throughout the country and their addresses are regularly published in the above magazines, in particular in People's Computer Company publications.

Computer stores are a new retailing phenomenon. Probably the first one was opened in Santa Monica, California, by Dick Heiser in the summer of 1975: the Arrowhead Computer Company. Shortly afterwards, the first Byte Shop was established in Mountain View,

California, by Paul Terrell. This shop led to a major chain of computer stores today.

Hundreds of stores that sell microcomputer systems and products exclusively, both to hobbyists and businesspeople, have opened in every major city in the U.S.A. and in Europe. Computer stores may offer valuable services: systems on display, repair and maintenance, special packages (both hardware and software), books, magazines, competent advice, classes and bulletin boards.

Selling general-purpose computers is reputed to call for skills not generally available in other retail stores, so that many of these specialized outlets are thriving. Even companies like IBM and Tandy have opened specialized computer stores.

A good computer store is a major advantage for comparative shopping, and for local assistance when getting started. However, the long term survival of many such ventures is not always assured.

CONSULTANTS

Traditionally, consultants have been a resource called upon for guidance in the selection and installation of large computer systems. Traditional consultants have, however, proved to be too costly (proportionately) for microcomputer systems users. The free consultant of today is the competent computer store owner or salesperson.

EDUCATION

Education is always the best investment prior to or, if necessary, after a purchase. A variety of media is available. Classes are often conducted at computer stores or universities, or by reputable commercial companies. Video programs are available from groups. Finally, books, or self-study courses are almost mandatory for an efficient selection and understanding.

COMPUTER SHOWS

The show that started it all was probably the Personal Computing Show organized in Atlantic City in August 1976 by John Dilks.

Organized in the tradition of radio hobbyists conventions, it was expected to attract a small number of visitors. Thousands came, and industry observers realized that a significant new trend was in motion: personal computing was a reality.

The success of this show triggered a wave of similar shows throughout the country. One of the highly successful ones on the West Coast has been the West Coast Computer Faire, organized by Jim Warren.

Computer shows provide a unique opportunity to view almost all available equipment at once, and conveniently obtain information and documentation. They are a highly valuable educational opportunity. Schedules are regularly published in microcomputer magazines.

OVERSEAS

A smaller number of microcomputer shops and specialized magazines now exist throughout the world. A useful reference in Europe is Euromicro, the European Association for Microprocessing. Computer shows are also organized in major countries, on a scale often comparable to that of the U.S.

MICROCOMPUTER MAGAZINES

BYTE
    70 Main Street
    Peterborough, New Hampshire 03458

COMPUTE
    P.O. Box 5119
    Greensboro, North Carolina 27403

CREATIVE COMPUTING
    P.O. Box 789-M
    Morristown, New Jersey

DR. DOBB'S JOURNAL
    Box 310
    Menlo Park, California 94025

80 MICROCOMPUTING
    80 Pine St.
    Petersborough, New Hampshire 03458

ELEMENTARY ELECTRONICS
    380 Lexington Avenue
    New York, New York 10017

EUROMICRO JOURNAL
Centre Paris Daumensil
4 Place Felix Eboue
75012 Paris, France

INFO WORLD
530 Lytton, Avenue
Palo Alto, California 94301

INTERFACE AGE
16704 Marquardt Avenue
Cerritos, California 90731

KILOBAUD MICROCOMPUTING
Pine Street
Peterborough, New Hampshire 03458

NIBBLE
Box 325
Lincoln, Massachusetts 01773

ON COMPUTING
70 Main Street
Peterborough, New Hampshire 03458

PEOPLE'S COMPUTERS
1263 El Camino Real, Box 5B
Menlo Park, California 94025

PERSONAL COMPUTING
1050 Commonwealth Avenue
Boston, Massachusetts 02215

SILICON GULCH GAZETTE
333 Swett Road
Woodside, California 94062

14

TOMORROW

CONCLUSION

Throughout this volume, all of the main concepts relating to micro-computers have been introduced. Additional technical information can be found in the Appendices.

The operation of a complete system and the detailed trade-offs for equipment selection should be clear, and the reader should have acquired all the knowledge necessary for a rational choice. The next step could be the purchase of a system for some actual practice (and enjoyment). Computer utilization might be considered the ultimate game, as it extends the functions of the user's intelligence and most users are quickly "hooked."

But this is a field that is expanding rapidly. What will the future bring?

TOMORROW

Prices and Miniaturization

With the cost of electronics continuing to decrease and miniaturization continuing to increase, it is likely that most mechanical or electro-mechanical components of today's systems will eventually become electronic. There will probably be a corresponding decrease in price and volume: we will have electronic keyboards, electronic displays and electronic mass memories. One-chip microcomputers are already available that have several thousand bytes of memory on the chip. Once certain boards have been standardized, they will become candidates for a one-chip implementation.

A complete system with today's functions could then be implemented within the volume of a pocket calculator, at a similar price. The main problem continues to be input-output at a human scale. This will probably remain the largest cost factor.

The computing function itself has become essentially free, so that an unlimited number of new applications can now be introduced. Will you develop one?

SUMMARY

Who would have predicted in 1975, the status of the field today? Although many speculations existed at that time, the reality has exceeded all expectations. This is the beginning of a new era, perhaps the "second industrial revolution." No one can predict even the short term future, in view of the explosive growth of this new industry.

Although not everyone will use microcomputers, everyone's life will eventually be changed by their use. One of your most valuable resources tomorrow will be as important as it is today: knowledge. This book should serve as a step along the path.

APPENDIX **A**

COMPUTER LOGIC

INTRODUCTION

This is a brief introduction to the basic concepts and symbols used for digital circuits in microcomputer systems.

All information is represented in binary format and processed, modified or transmitted by these circuits.

THE BASIC LOGIC CIRCUITS

The basic logic circuits are AND, OR and NOR, with some variations, such as XOR, NAND, and NOT. They are used in combinations, to provide all other functions.

The function of each "gate" is represented by a truth table (see Figure A-1).

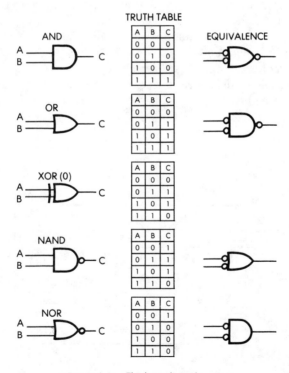

Figure A-1:   The basic logic functions

For example, the output "C" of an AND gate will be "1" only if both "A" and "B" are "1". Otherwise, the output will be "0".

Similarly, the output "C" of an OR gate will be "1" if either or both of the inputs "A" or "B" are "1".

Flip-Flops

We also need some memory devices that will memorize a state ("0" or "1") and change state when told to.

The various flip-flops appear in Figures A-2 and A-3.

— A "D flip-flop" introduces a delay. Inputs are always complementary.

— A "J-K flip-flop" modulates its response in function of the combination of inputs (see truth table). The output Q is "clocked," and changes only after the clock pulse.

— An "R-S flip-flop" is a Set-Reset flip-flop—the simplest. It is a *latch*, set when Q = 1, asynchronous or synchronous (if clock is used).

The possible implementations of the flip-flops with elementary gates appear in Figure A-4.

A *register* is a set of latches (8 for a byte).

Finally, miscellaneous electronic and electrical symbols appear in Figures A-5 and A-6.

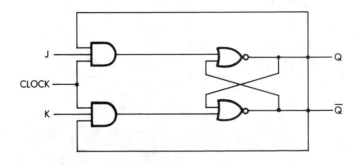

Figure A-2: A J-K flip-flop

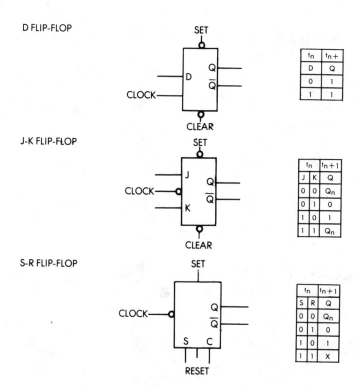

D FLIP-FLOP

t_n	t_n+
D	Q
0	1
1	1

J-K FLIP-FLOP

t_n		t_n+1
J	K	Q
0	0	Q_n
0	1	0
1	0	1
1	1	Q_n

S-R FLIP-FLOP

t_n		t_n+1
S	R	Q
0	0	Q_n
0	1	0
1	0	1
1	1	X

Figure A-3:   Flip-flop

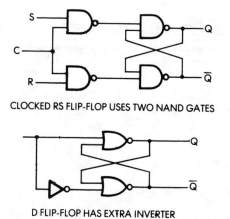

CLOCKED RS FLIP-FLOP USES TWO NAND GATES

D FLIP-FLOP HAS EXTRA INVERTER

Figure A-4:   Flip-flops with gates

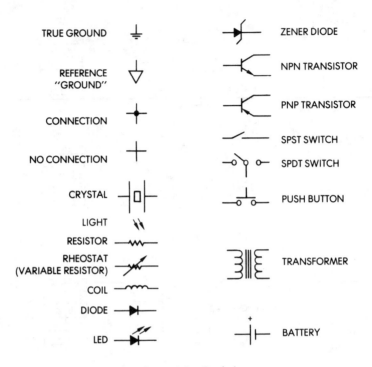

Figure A-5: Symbols

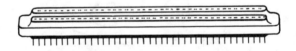

Figure A-6: An edge connector

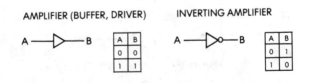

Figure A-7: Amplifiers

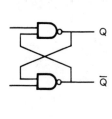

Figure A-8: Latch

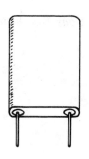

Figure A-9: Crystal

EXERCISES

Exercise: *What is the name of the gate implemented by the following circuit?*

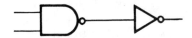

Answer: AND

Exercise: *Construct the truth table for a 3-input AND gate:*

Answer:

A	B	C	Q
0	0	0	0
0	0	1	0
0	1	0	0
0	1	1	0
1	0	0	0
1	0	1	0
1	1	0	0
1	1	1	1

Exercise: *Construct the truth table for a 3-input NAND gate:*

Answer:

A	B	C	Q
0	0	0	1
0	0	1	1
0	1	0	1
0	1	1	1
1	0	0	1
1	0	1	1
1	1	0	1
1	1	1	0

APPENDIX **B**

BITS AND BYTES

THE BINARY SYSTEM

This chapter is a brief introduction to the binary system used inside the computer to represent information. In principle, numbers are simple to represent. The binary representation uses 0's and 1's to represent all numbers. Let us look at some examples:

3 is represented by 11

5 is represented by 101

The decimal equivalent is computed as follows:

11 is $1 \times 2 + 1 \times 1 = 3$

101 is $1 \times 4 + 0 \times 2 + 1 \times 1 = 5$

The rightmost bit (binary digit) represents $2° = 1$. It is called the "least significant bit" (LSB). Going from right to left, as in the decimal system, each successive bit represents a corresponding power of 2. Thus, in "101", the rightmost bit represents 1, the next one $2^1 = 2$, and the next one $2^2 = 4$.

We know now how to obtain the decimal equivalent: If $b_n b_{n-1}...b_1 b_0$ is the binary number, its decimal equivalent is:

$b_n \times 2^n + b_{n-1} \times 2^{n-1} + b_1 \times 2 + b_0$

where the b's are 0's or 1's.

FROM DECIMAL TO BINARY

The reverse conversion is just as simple:

16 divided by 2 is 8, remainder is 0

8 divided by 2 is 4, remainder is 0

4 divided by 2 is 2, remainder is 0

2 divided by 2 is 1, remainder is 0

The last quotient, plus the remainders, are, bottom up: 10000. This is "16".

Another example:
11 divided by 2 is 5, remainder is 1
 5 divided by 2 is 2, remainder is 1
 2 divided by 2 is 1, remainder is 0
The answer is 1011.

Exercise: *Convert 10000 and 1011 to decimal in order to verify the previous conversions.*

NUMBER REPRESENTATIONS

We have now shown that decimal numbers may be represented by bits. In practice, current microcomputers structure all information in groups of 8 bits, or bytes.

Exercise: *What is the largest integer that a byte may represent?*

Answer: $2^8 = 256$

Exercise: *What is the largest integer that two bytes may represent?*

Answer: $2^{16} = 65,536 = 64K$

Binary Arithmetic
Arithmetic operations are performed in the same manner as in the decimal system:

```
    0101      (5)
+   0110      (6)
=   1011      (11)
```

The rules of addition are expressed by:
        0 + 0 = 0
        0 + 1 = 1
        1 + 0 = 1
        1 + 1 = 10 (or "0" with a carry of "1")

Negative and Fractional Numbers

The next problems are to represent negative numbers and fractional numbers.

Briefly, signed numbers are generally represented in the "two's complement notation," while fractional numbers require a "floating-point" representation.

CHARACTERS

Characters are (almost) universally encoded in ASCII 8-bit code. The ASCII conversion table appears in Chapter 5.

Seven bits may be encoded $2^7 = 128$ different characters. This is sufficient for:

26 letters of the alphabet (A through Z), upper case
26 letters of the alphabet (a through z), lower case
10 decimal digits (0 through 9)
66 special symbols.

Additional characters are almost never required. For this reason, the ASCII code is used universally. In practice, several "characters" are control characters, which do not print, and are used as commands or status information between the computer and the terminal. For example, ESC(ape) is generally used as a "STOP THIS" command.

Question: *What is the eighth bit used for?*

Answer: It is the *parity* bit.

Let us now illustrate the use of the binary system on a final example:

The user types "THIS IS 12".

The monitor or the editor program will capture these characters from the keyboard and store them in the memory in binary form. Let us assume that the code for:

SPACE is 10100000
T   is 11010100
H   is 01001000
I   is 11001001
S   is 01010011
1   is 10110001
2   is 10110010

The representation of the string "THIS IS 12" is:

11010100
01001000
11001001
01010011
10100000
11001001
01010011
10100000
10110001
10110010

Question: *Isn't there an error in the representation of 12?*

Answer: No. When digits appear in a "string," they are treated as ASCII characters, and "12" is represented by the ASCII character for "1", followed by the ASCII character for "2". An Editor program does not know about numbers. It manipulates only characters. If an "assembler" is used, it will have to "know" that a number is a number, usually by finding it on the right of an operator, such as =, +, or −. It will then encode the number in binary (usually two's complement), so that it can easily perform binary arithmetic on it.

Question for the thorough reader: *What element of the system (hardware and software) performs the conversion from the key closure on the keyboard to the actual byte that represents the character: 1 - the microprocessor, 2 - the keyboard encoder?*

Answer: If the keyboard has an encoder (alphanumeric keyboards normally do), then the encoder does. Otherwise (small 16 or 24-key keyboards are usually "naked"), a conversion program does the encoding (it is part of the "monitor" program).

BASIC COMPUTER COMMUNICATIONS

PARALLEL AND SERIAL

Four main options exist for transmitting information between a computer and its peripherals: parallel vs. serial, and synchronous vs. asynchronous.

Parallel

Parallel transmission, in the case of a standard microcomputer, involves 8 bits, i.e., an 8-wire "bus." Parallel transmission is faster than serial transmission, where bits are transmitted one after the other. Whenever speed is required, parallel transmission should be used.

Parallel transmission is used inside the microcomputer where boards must exchange information at the highest possible speed. The bus, which runs on the *motherboard* and carries signals between the boards is, therefore, always parallel. This is the case with the S-100 bus, already described.

Outside the microcomputer, a parallel bus requires 8 lines for data, plus many control lines, for synchronization signals. These signals are required to perform input-output operations between devices that operate at different speeds. In particular, a parallel bus is required for a (high-speed) parallel printer.

Serial

Serial transmission consists of sending bits on a single line one after the other. In order to distinguish between two successive bits, a "clock" signal is also required. The obvious advantage is the low cost of the communication line (just two wires). However, in view of the limited bandwidth available for reliable transmission, this technique limits the speed of transmission. Also, it requires an 8-bit buffer at each end to accumulate a character. Serial transmission is simple and economical, and is used for most "slow peripherals," such as Teletypewriters and

CRT terminals. The usable speed varies from 110 baud to 9600 baud. In the digital world, a baud is a bit per second, or bps. Note that a Teletype is a 110 baud terminal (10 characters per second, using 11 bits each). A Decwriter LA 36 is a 300 baud terminal. A standard CRT operates at 9600 + baud.

Serial Interfaces

The two most often used standard serial interfaces are RS-232C and the 20mA current loop. The 20mA is the usual Teletype interface, where "Mark" is 1 and "Space" is 0.

RS-232C is used by CRTs, slow printers, and for telephone connections. + 3 to + 15V are used for "0", and − 3 to − 15V are used for "1".

SYNCHRONOUS AND ASYNCHRONOUS

Information may be sent one byte at a time: this is an *asynchronous* technique. However, the terminal "never knows" when a character arrives. In order for the computer to recognize a character, some synchronization information must travel with the character.

Thus, the Teletype uses an ASCII 8-bit code for the character, preceded by a "START" bit, and terminated by two " STOP" bits. This is why a 10 cps (character per second) Teletype requires 110 baud: each character requires 11 bits.

Asynchronous communication is used wherever possible, as it is simple and reliable. Synchronous transmission sends "packets" or blocks of data, which must be carefully synchronized. It offers the potential of high speed, but requires substantially more logic, and is, therefore, more costly. It may be used, for example, for high speed communication with another computer.

BEYOND THE MICROCOMPUTER SYSTEM

A microcomputer may communicate with distant peripherals (or other microcomputers) over telephone lines (or, for short distances, via a twisted pair). In order for information to be reliably transmitted for long distances over telephone lines, the information must be encoded into audible frequencies (in serial form). This is done by a modem.

A *modem* is a modulator-demodulator. It encodes the serial binary data into frequencies and decodes frequencies into serial bits. The most commonly used technique is FSK, or "Frequency-Shift-Keying": a median frequency is used as the "carrier." This frequency indicates a "no data transmitted" state. When data is transmitted, this frequency is shifted up or down. A "1" is pulsed by sending a higher frequency ("shifting" it up). A "0" is pulsed by sending a lower frequency.

One frequency may be used to send; another frequency, well-separated from the first, may receive. A communication in which data may be sent in both directions is said to be "full-duplex." Otherwise, it is "half-duplex."

For high transmission speeds, higher-quality telephone lines may be leased. This is the way in which larger computers are tied into networks.

SUMMARY

Inside the microcomputer box, all information transfers are normally parallel.

Outside the box, transfers are serial, via an RS-232C connector or a 20mA current loop to slow terminals, and parallel, via specialized ports and connectors to high-speed devices.

The microcomputer may also communicate via telephone lines by using a modem.

FILES AND RECORDS

STORING INFORMATION

A *file* is an information unit created by the user (or a program). A file may be a program, a mailing list, or an accounts receivable list. The user must assign a name to every file he/she uses. For example, the user might type:

"LOAD (FROM THE DISK) PAYROLL"

PAYROLL is the name of the file to be transferred from the disk into the memory. Files can be very different as to their size and contents. A file can have any length and can grow or decrease in size.

Files also present many practical design problems and require a good "file system" program. For example, it is important that:

— Information in the middle of the file can be accessed efficiently.
— Information about the file is available (e.g., its length, or its nature such as binary or ASCII).
— The contents of a file remain correct and secure.

In order to avoid these problems, techniques have evolved that have resulted in a variety of design options for "structured files." Let us review the main techniques.

STORAGE ALLOCATION

Every file may normally vary in size. A "payroll" file, for example, will typically grow, and sometimes decrease in size. However, every storage medium, whether disk or tape, is finite. The most straightforward way to handle this situation is to allocate an entire diskette, or an entire tape to the file, thus making sure that the file will have plenty of room to grow. Unfortunately only one (or two) tapes or diskettes are usually connected to the system at any time. Such a solution "wastes space," i.e., restricts the number of files that the user will be able to access simultaneously. (There is only one file per storage device.)

An obvious improvement is to define a maximum length for the file (e.g., half a cassette tape). This way, there can be several files per cassette (two in our case). However, if the file remains small, this solution will again waste most of the space available.

Sequential Files

From a space usage standpoint, it would be best to store files "sequentially," i.e., one after the other. Unfortunately, if one file grows, then all the others must be moved, or else the next one will have to be removed. This is a lengthy and cumbersome process.

This problem is particularly important in the case of tape systems which can only be accessed sequentially. The simplest solution, often used, consists of allowing a file to grow on the tape or cassette, and moving other programs to another tape. This solution does, however, waste storage space, and alternatives have been devices, such as records and blocks.

The other disadvantage is an access problem: access is essentially sequential. It is difficult to retrieve information at random intervals.

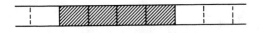

Figure D-1:   A sequential file

Records and Blocks

In order to facilitate the allocation of storage to a file, most "file systems" structure available storage in blocks. These blocks may be of equal size, or of varying sizes. In most cases, they are of equal size, for simplicity. We will now assume that these blocks are of equal size. They will be called "sectors," "pages," or "records," depending upon the system.

A file will now use several blocks, one of which (the last one) will usually not be full. Then, on the average, only half a block of storage is wasted. How does the file grow? Quite simply, one or more blocks, if available, are allocated to the file.

The next problem is how to keep track of all the blocks allocated to the file, as they are not likely to be in sequence.

Structuring a File

Two basic structures may be used: a *directory* or a *linked list*.

A Directory

In a directory structure, a "directory block" (or a directory file, using several blocks) contains the *"pointers"* (addresses) of all the blocks belonging to the file.

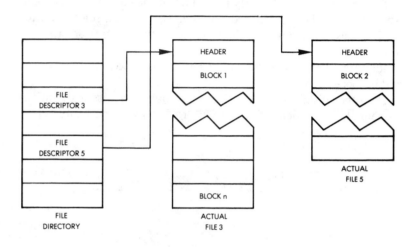

Figure D-2: A directory structure

For example, on a diskette, the directory for file **"PAYROLL"** contains:

    1 - 2
    1 - 3
    1 - 4
    2 - 5

This may be read as:

    first block is sector 2 of track 1
    next block is sector 3 of track 1
    next block is sector 4 of track 1
    next block is sector 5 of track 2

This is a simple and straightforward way to structure a file. However, to be efficient, this method requires that the directory be read and that it reside in the central memory of the computer. At the end of every block, the directory must be accessed to determine which is the next block to be accessed.

Exercise: *How can the file system keep track of available blocks, so that it can allocate one or release one (or more)?*

Answer: Inspect Figure D-3 for the answer.

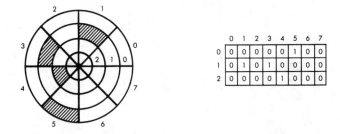

Figure D-3:   A bit map may be used for disk sector management

Linked List

An alternative is to store information in each block. This is illustrated in Figure D-4. Each block contains a "pointer" to the next block belonging to the file. A special marker, "EOF" (End of File) indicates the end of the linked list.

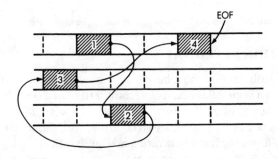

Figure D-4:   Linked blocks

Indexed Sequential

Hybrid methods may be used, such as a directory (an "index") of sequential files. This is called indexed sequential access, a notable improvement over simple sequential access.

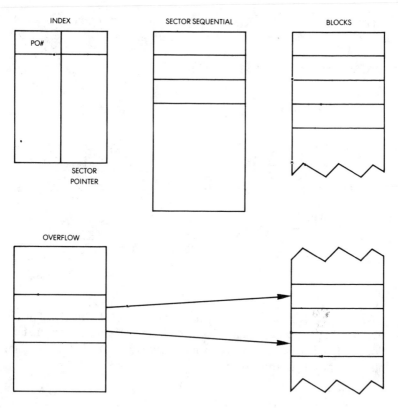

Figure D-5:   Storing P.O.s using indexed sequential retrieval

INFORMATION RETRIEVAL

The next problem that must be solved is how to access information efficiently. In a sequential file, it is necessary to read a complete file in order to access any of its elements. This method is very slow.

The problem can be solved, by structuring. The more efficient the access mechanism, the more structuring is required. Structuring usually means successive directories, or complex chaining, and results in a longer *minimum* access time. It reduces the *average* access time.

Trees

One of the simplest ways to structure files is to use a *tree* structure. A master directory contains pointers to subdirectories, and so on, up to the actual file. In order to retrieve a file, one must "walk through the tree."

Other structures may be used to store information, and to manage blocks within the file itself. However, they are beyond the scope of this book.

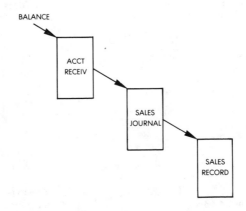

Figure D-6:   A tree of business lists

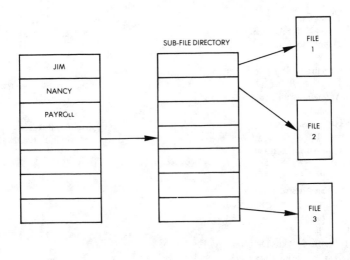

Figure D-7:   A two-level directory tree

SMALL BUSINESS SYSTEM MANUFACTURERS

Basic Four
2500 Wilshire Boulevard
Los Angeles, California 90057

Burroughs
Burroughs Place
Detroit, Michigan 48232

Data General
4400 Computer Drive
Westboro, Massachusetts 01580

Datapoint
9725 Datapoint Drive
San Antonio, Texas 78284

Digital Equipment Corporation
146 Main Street
Maynard, Massachusetts 01754

Four Phase Systems
10700 N. De Anza Boulevard
Cupertino, California 95014

General Automation
1055 S. East Street
Anaheim, California 92805

Hewlett Packard
1507 Page Mill Road
Palo Alto, California 94314

Honeywell
200 Smith Street
Waltham, Massachusetts 02154

IBM
General Systems Division
4111 Northside Parkway
Atlanta, Georgia 30301

Logical Machine
P.O. Box 60249
Sunnyvale, California 94086

Microdata
17481 Red Hill Avenue
Irvine, California 92705

NCR
Dayton, Ohio 45479

Olivetti
500 Park Avenue
New York, New York 10022

Phillips Business Systems
810 Woodbury Road
Woodbury, New York 11797

Qantel
3525 Breakwater Avenue
Hayward, California 94545

Sycor
100 Phoenix Drive
Ann Arbor, Michigan 48104

Wang
1 Industrial Avenue
Lowell, Massachusetts 01851

MICROCOMPUTER MANUFACTURERS

Alpha Microsystems
17881 Sky Park North
Irvine, California 92714

Altos Computer Systems
2360 Bering Drive
San Jose, California 95131

Apple Computer
10260 Bandley Drive
Cupertino, California 95014

Atari
1265 Borregas Avenue
Sunnyvale, California 94086

Bally
2640 W. Belmont Avenue
Chicago, Illinois 60618

Commodore Business Systems
3330 Scott Boulevard
Santa Clara, California 95051

Compucolor
Intecolor Drive
225 Technology Park
Norcross, Georgia 30092

Cromemco
280 Bernardo Avenue
Mountain View, California 94040

Data General
Westboro, Massachusetts 01580

Digital Group
P.O. Box 6528
Denver, Colorado 80206

Digital Microsystems
4448 Piedmont Avenue
Oakland, California 94611

Dynabyte
115 Independence Drive
Menlo Park, California 94025

E & L Instruments, Inc.
61 First Street
Derby, Connecticut 06418

Exidy, Inc.
390 Java Drive
Sunnyvale, California 94086

Extensys
404 Tasman Drive
Sunnyvale, California 94086

Heath
Benton Harbor, Michigan 49022

Industrial Micro Systems
628 N. Eckhoff Street
Orange, California 92688

Ithaca Intersystems
1650 Hanshaw Road
P.O. Box 91
Ithaca, New York 14850

Logical Machines
P.O. Box 60249
Sunnyvale, California 94086

Mattel
5150 W. Rosecrans
Hawthorne, California 90250

MOS Technology
950 Rittonhouse Road
Norristown, Pennsylvania 19401

Midwest Scientific Instruments
220 W. Cedar
Olathe, Kansas 66061

North Star Computers
1440 Fourth Street
Berkeley, California 94710

Ohio Scientific
1333 S. Chillicothe Road
Aurora, Ohio 44202

Percom Data Computers
211 N. Kirby
Garland, Texas 75042

Polymorphic Systems
460 Ward Drive
Santa Barbara, California 93111

Radio Shack
1300 One Tandy Center
Fort Worth, Texas 76102

SD Sales
3401 W. Kingsley
Garland, Texas 75041

Southwest Technical Products
219 W. Rhapsody
San Antonio, Texas 78216

Synertek Systems
3001 Stender Way
Santa Clara, California 95051

Umtech
2950 Patrick Henry Drive
Santa Clara, California 95050

Xitan
Research Park
Building H
1101 State Road
Princeton, New Jersey 08540

Index

The SYBEX Library

BASIC PROGRAMS FOR SCIENTISTS AND ENGINEERS
by **Alan R. Miller** 340 pp., 120 illustr., Ref. B240
This second book in the "Programs for Scientists and Engineers" series provides a library of problem solving programs while developing proficiency in BASIC.

INSIDE BASIC GAMES
by **Richard Mateosian** 350 pp., 240 Illustr., Ref. B245
Teaches interactive BASIC programming through games. Games are written in Microsoft BASIC and can run on the TRS-80, APPLE II and PET/CBM.

FIFTY BASIC EXERCISES
by **J.P. Lamoitier** 240 pp., 195 Illustr., Ref. B250
Teaches BASIC by actual practice using graduated exercises drawn from everyday applications. All programs written in Microsoft BASIC.

EXECUTIVE PLANNING WITH BASIC
by **X.T. Bui** 192 pp., 19 illustr., Ref. B380
An important collection of business management decision models in BASIC, including Inventory Management (EOQ), Critical Path Analysis and PERT, Financial Ratio Analysis, Portfolio Management, and much more.

BASIC FOR BUSINESS
by **Douglas Hergert** 250 pp., 15 illustr., Ref. B390
A logically organized, no-nonsense introduction to BASIC programming for business applications. Includes many fully explained accounting programs, and shows you how to write them.

BASIC EXERCISES FOR THE APPLE
by **J.P. Lamoitier** 230 pp., 80 illustr., Ref. B500
For all Apple users, this learn-by-doing book is written in APPLESOFT II BASIC. Exercises have been chosen for their educational value and application to math, physics, games, business, accounting, and statistics.

YOUR FIRST COMPUTER
by **Rodnay Zaks** 260 pp., 150 Illustr., Ref. C200A
The most popular introduction to small computers and their peripherals: what they do and how to buy one.

DON'T (or How to Care for Your Computer)
by **Rodnay Zaks** 220 pp., 100 Illustr., Ref. C400
The correct way to handle and care for all elements of a computer system including what to do when something doesn't work.

INTRODUCTION TO WORD PROCESSING
by **Hal Glatzer** 200 pp., 70 illustr., Ref. W101
Explains in plain language what a word processor can do, how it improves productivity, how to use a word processor and how to buy one wisely.

INTRODUCTION TO WORDSTAR
by **Arthur Naiman** 200 pp., 30 illustr., Ref. W105
Makes it easy to learn how to use WordStar, a powerful word processing program for personal computers.

FROM CHIPS TO SYSTEMS: AN INTRODUCTION TO MICROPROCESSORS
by **Rodnay Zaks**   560 pp., 255 illustr., Ref. C201A
A simple and comprehensive introduction to microprocessors from both a hardware and software standpoint: what they are, how they operate, how to assemble them into a complete system.

MICROPROCESSOR INTERFACING TECHNIQUES
by **Rodnay Zaks and Austin Lesea**   460 pp., 400 Illustr., Ref. C207
Complete hardware and software interconnect techniques including D to A conversion, peripherals, standard buses and troubleshooting.

PROGRAMMING THE 6502
by **Rodnay Zaks**   390 pp., 160 Illustr., Ref. C202
Assembly language programming for the 6502, from basic concepts to advanced data structures.

6502 APPLICATIONS BOOK
by **Rodnay Zaks**   280 pp., 205 Illustr., Ref. D302
Real life application techniques: the input/output book for the 6502.

ADVANCED 6502 PROGRAMMING
by **Rodnay Zaks**   300 pp., 140 Illustr., Ref. G402A
Third in the 6502 series. Teaches more advanced programming techniques, using games as a framework for learning.

PROGRAMMING THE Z80
by **Rodnay Zaks**   620 pp., 200 Illustr., Ref. C280
A complete course in programming the Z80 microprocessor and a thorough introduction to assembly language.

PROGRAMMING THE Z8000
by **Richard Mateosian**   300 pp., 125 Illustr., Ref. C281
How to program the Z8000 16-bit microprocessor. Includes a description of the architecture and function of the Z8000 and its family of support chips.

THE CP/M HANDBOOK (with MP/M)
by **Rodnay Zaks**   330 pp., 100 Illustr., Ref. C300
An indispensable reference and guide to CP/M—the most widely used operating system for small computers.

INTRODUCTION TO PASCAL (Including UCSD PASCAL)
by **Rodnay Zaks**   420 pp., 130 Illustr., Ref. P310
A step-by-step introduction for anyone wanting to learn the Pascal language. Describes UCSD and Standard Pascals. No technical background is assumed.

THE PASCAL HANDBOOK
by **Jacques Tiberghien**   490 pp., 350 Illustr., Ref. P320
A dictionary of the Pascal language, defining every reserved word, operator, procedure and function found in all major versions of Pascal.

PASCAL PROGRAMS FOR SCIENTISTS AND ENGINEERS
by **Alan Miller**   400 pp., 80 Illustr., Ref. P340
A comprehensive collection of frequently used algorithms for scientific and technical applications, programmed in Pascal. Includes such programs as curve-fitting, integrals and statistical techniques.

APPLE PASCAL GAMES
by Douglas Hergert and Joseph T. Kalash   380 pp., 40 illustr., Ref. P360
A collection of the most popular computer games in Pascal challenging the reader not only to play but to investigate how games are implemented on the computer.

INTRODUCTION TO THE UCSD p-SYSTEM
by Charles T. Grant and Jon Butah   320 pp., 110 illustr., Ref. P370
A simple, clear introduction to the UCSD Pascal Operating System for beginners through experienced programmers.

INTERNATIONAL MICROCOMPUTER DICTIONARY
140 pp., Ref. X2
All the definitions and acronyms of microcomputer jargon defined in a handy pocket-size edition. Includes translations of the most popular terms into ten languages.

MICROPROGRAMMED APL IMPLEMENTATION
by Rodnay Zaks   350 pp., Ref. Z10
An expert-level text presenting the complete conceptual analysis and design of an APL interpreter, and actual listings of the microcode.

SELF STUDY COURSES

Recorded live at seminars given by recognized professionals in the microprocessor field.

INTRODUCTORY SHORT COURSES:
Each includes two cassettes plus special coordinated workbook (2½ hours).

S10—INTRODUCTION TO PERSONAL AND BUSINESS COMPUTING
A comprehensive introduction to small computer systems for those planning to use or buy one, including peripherals and pitfalls.

S1—INTRODUCTION TO MICROPROCESSORS
How microprocessors work, including basic concepts, applications, advantages and disadvantages.

S2—PROGRAMMING MICROPROCESSORS
The companion to S1. How to program any standard microprocessor, and how it operates internally. Requires a basic understanding of microprocessors.

S3—DESIGNING A MICROPROCESSOR SYSTEM
Learn how to interconnect a complete system, wire by wire. Techniques discussed are applicable to all standard microprocessors.

INTRODUCTORY COMPREHENSIVE COURSES:
Each includes a 300-500 page seminar book and seven or eight C90 cassettes.

SB3—MICROPROCESSORS
This seminar teaches all aspects of microprocessors: from the operation of an MPU to the complete interconnect of a system. The basic hardware course (12 hours).

SB2—MICROPROCESSOR PROGRAMMING
The basic software course: step by step through all the important aspects of microcomputer programming (10 hours).

ADVANCED COURSES:
Each includes a 300-500 page workbook and three or four C90 cassettes.

SB3—SEVERE ENVIRONMENT/MILITARY MICROPROCESSOR SYSTEMS
Complete discussion of constraints, techniques and systems for severe environmental applications, including Hughes, Raytheon, Actron and other militarized systems (6 hours).

SB5—BIT-SLICE
Learn how to build a complete system with bit slices. Also examines innovative applications of bit slice techniques (6 hours).

SB6—INDUSTRIAL MICROPROCESSOR SYSTEMS
Seminar examines actual industrial hardware and software techniques, components, programs and cost (4½ hours).

SB7—MICROPROCESSOR INTERFACING
Explains how to assemble, interface and interconnect a system (6 hours).

FOR A COMPLETE CATALOG
OF OUR PUBLICATIONS

U.S.A	SYBEX-EUROPE	SYBEX-VERLAG
2344 Sixth Street	4 Place Félix-Eboué	Heyestr. 22
Berkeley,	75583 Paris Cedex 12	4000 Düsseldorf 12
California 94710	France	West Germany
Tel: (415) 848-8233	Tel: 1/347-30-20	Tel: (0211) 287066
Telex: 336311	Telex: 211801	Telex: 08 588 163